Haskins

The Bear Facts

Haskins

The Bear Facts

as told to
RAY SANCHEZ

With an Introductory Note
By Jay Ambrose

MANGAN BOOKS
and
EL PASO HERALD-POST
El Paso, Texas

To
My wife Mary, my four sons,
My late father, my mother and brother
And all my former and present players.

—Don Haskins

To
My son Victor
Who loves the game.

—Ray Sanchez

An Introductory Note

I was born and raised in Kentucky, which is to say, I am somebody who sometimes behaves as if basketball outranks God, country and family as the most important thing in life. In that basketball-crazy state, chroniclers have noted few years in which enthusiasm for the sport was more contagious than 1966. That was the year of "Rupp's Runts," the small but very good team coached by the legendary Adolph Rupp at the University of Kentucky. I was a senior that year at a small college called Transylvania, which happens to be located in Lexington, the home of the UK Wildcats. On Saturdays, I and other guys in my dormitory would gather around a TV set and whoop and cheer as the Runts, with finesse and pretty shooting, would destroy some group of giants. Like little kids anticipating a ton of toys from Santa on Christmas, we began to dream that "it" would happen; maybe, just maybe, the university was on its way to another national championship. And in fact, those UK kids did work their way to the final NCAA game. But something funny happened on their way to the Christmas tree. Some little school from out of nowhere whipped us, some school none of us had heard of, a school called Texas Western. Not only did Texas Western win, but it won convincingly — and through quickness, by stealing the ball from UK's finesse players. The Texas boys made the Kentucky boys look like clods.

I graduated, got in the newspaper business and took jobs in such varied places as a couple of Kentucky towns, Albany, New York, and Denver, Colorado. In 1983, I joined the *El Paso Herald-Post*. I asked somebody right after arriving here whether the University of Texas at El Paso had a decent basketball team. Decent? It has a great team, came the response. Why, in 1966, before the school changed its name, I was told, the team won the NCAA tournament. It was only then that I realized that I had come to inhabit the same city as the beast of one of my nightmares. It was not long, however, before I became a fan of the beast, better known as the Miners. I began going to the games and discovered that UTEP played a stylish game, with emphasis on hard work, quickness, teamwork, intelligent strategy, intensity and defense. The reason for the continued excellence soon became clear to me. UTEP has one of the best basketball coaches in the nation, the man this book is about. He is Don Haskins, The Bear.

Haskins is one of the most celebrated figures in El Paso, as much a legend in this part of the country as Rupp was in Kentucky. He should be. His accomplishments are as extraordinary as his bigger-than-life personality. It's not easy to compile winning seasons in college basketball or repeatedly to win conference titles. It is enormously difficult to win a national title. The schools that do reach that pinnacle usually boast lavishly funded programs that get tons of publicity. They are able to attract the most highly touted athletes coming out of high school. El Paso is geographically isolated. It is not in the path of the Eastern-based media and cannot offer the athletes splendid accommodations and immediate

10

national reputations. Nevertheless, Haskins has been able to find good players and has been able to teach them how to play the game the Haskins way, which is a winning way. He has given this city — a rather poor, sometimes forgotten city that has known and still knows hard times — more than a little to brag about.

Haskins' nickname is no accident. He's a bear of a man physically — but also emotionally. Watch him on the bench during a game and what you see is total absorption in the task at hand. Here is not just a bear. Here is a thunderstorm, now quiet, then suddenly crackling with lightning. Don Haskins directing his team is almost as much fun to watch as the team itself. Don Haskins, the human being, is fun to learn about as well, for he is a generous, good-spirited man who values the fundamental things, the virtues of determination and sticking with a job until it's done and done right.

The author of this book is my friend Ray Sanchez, sports editor of the *El Paso Herald-Post*, and I can think of no one better equipped to tell the Haskins story. A native of El Paso, Ray went to UTEP and has been writing about sports in the city for more than thirty years. Ray, who brings insight and finely honed writing skills to this book, tells you things about Haskins you never heard before. You will see sides of him you did not know existed. You will learn about the man and about the wonders of that ceaselessly fascinating game of basketball.

And you will learn about an important aspect of El Paso history. Sports, after all, are not just games. Sports are drama and celebration. Sports help us cohere as a community. Athletes are our warriors, doing non-lethal battle on our behalf, relieving us from tedium and sometimes providing

11

us with exhilaration. At their best, athletes are also artists; I have seen gargantuan, hugely muscled basketball players fly through the air with as much impromptu grace as any ballet dancer's plotted grace. Athletes, and our involvement in their struggles, help define what we are. In ways that are subtle and not so subtle, they both reflect and shape our society.

So read and learn and enjoy, as I read and learned and enjoyed, even though The Bear once stole my Christmas.

Jay Ambrose, editor of *El Paso Herald-Post*

Preface

It was love at first sound.

I was sitting at my desk in the sports department of the *El Paso Herald-Post* one day in 1961 when a tall young man walked in.

"Hi," he said. "I'm Don Haskins, the new basketball coach at Texas Western College. Let's go have a beer."

Now how can you help but like someone with an introduction like that? Here was a down-to-earth guy, a fellow who wasn't going to wait for the world to come to him but was going out to meet the world head-on. I foresaw good things ahead for the young man and the school.

And I was right.

I accepted the invitation, and a relationship began that, while not close all these years, has certainly been a joyous one. I saw him become one of the greatest coaches in the history of the game, win a national championship in 1966, win an unprecedented five Western Athletic Conference championships in a row.

I watched as he single-handedly turned the sleepy little town of El Paso into a cheering, applauding, vibrant community that can't wait for basketball season to roll around each year. And I saw him bring national recognition to the city that was beyond its wildest dreams.

13

This point in his life is perfect for this book. It comes after his twenty-sixth year as coach of the Miners, who now play under the banner of University of Texas at El Paso, and after his fifth consecutive WAC title.

Haskins, as his introduction to this writer shows, is a friendly sort. And a kindly man. He's gone out of his way to help many a person on numerous occasions. And he's always made himself available to the news media.

But he's a private person in some ways. He hates to speak at public functions, or have anyone make a big show of his triumphs. He's big and growls a lot on the basketball court, thus his nickname of "The Bear." But away from the court, he's a shy and modest person.

In his first twenty-six years with the Miners, Haskins has won 493 games and lost a mere 215. He ranks among the top eight winningest coaches of all time in college ranks.

You'll find a list of some of his accomplishments in the back of this book. I put them in myself. Haskins wasn't about to do it.

Because of his retiring nature, this book is significant in more than the usual sense. He tells not only of his experiences on the basketball court, but about his private life. The myths, untruths and non-facts that have appeared from time to time are set straight.

And the book is instructional. You can find out what made young men like Nate Archibald such great players. And you'll learn a lot about coaching.

Here, you'll hear it straight from the horse's mouth.

Or maybe I should say, straight from The Bear's mouth.

Ray Sanchez

One

I'VE BEEN CALLED a champion of civil rights. It's been said I've been a crusader for blacks. Pat Riley, the coach of the Los Angeles Lakers, has been quoted as saying I took part in the Emancipation Proclamation of 1966.

But nothing like that was on my mind when I started five blacks on our Texas Western College team against University of Kentucky in the finals of the NCAA basketball tournament that year. If it advanced opportunities for blacks and if it showed the world what they could do, well and good. But I started the five players I thought would have the best chance of beating Kentucky. That they were all black and that it was the first time five black players had started in an NCAA finals was strictly incidental to me.

Not much of the black-versus-white issue was made in the media nor in conversations I heard during the Final Four tournament. Most of the first reports of our 72–65 victory over the all-white Kentucky team made little mention of racial issues.

It wasn't until several days later that the issue hit me. And it wasn't pretty.

I received thousands of letters within the next few weeks. All but a few were what you would call hate mail. They'd bring the letters into my office in wastebaskets, and I guess that was appropriate. That's where they belonged.

15

The letters usually started with "nigger lover" or some such term. Most of them came from the South — from states like Louisiana, Georgia, Mississippi and, of course, Kentucky.

I even got some from parts of Texas despite the fact we were the only Texas team ever to win an NCAA basketball championship. The letters weren't from West Texas but from East Texas.

I find it ironic that teams in the states from which most of the hate letters were received are now predominantly black.

Ugly things were said in the national press, too, although more subtly. The eligibility of our center, David Lattin, was questioned. The NCAA came down to investigate. They wanted to know if he had a high school diploma. He did, of course.

Sports Illustrated ran an article months later which hurt our recruiting for years. The point of the article was that we "exploited" blacks. It said none of the players' wives could get a job in El Paso. That was true. None of the players was married!

The story started out quoting our athletic director at the time, George McCarty. The writer stated McCarty used the phrase "our nigger athletes."

Not true. I was in the room at the time McCarty was supposed to have said that. So was football coach Bobby Dobbs, sports information director Eddie Mullens and track coach Wayne Vandenburg.

We lost a lot of players because of that article. Coaches competing with us for athletes would carry that issue of *Sports Illustrated* in their hip pockets and show them to recruits. That went on for years. It got so that sometimes I wished we had never won the national championship.

Two

MORE ABOUT the 1966 team later, but for now let me say that basketball didn't come easy to me. In fact, what success I have achieved is due to sheer stubbornness.

I was born in Enid, Oklahoma on March 14, 1930. We were neither poor nor rich. My father, Paul, was my idol. He was sort of a frustrated jock. He was a great athlete but he never had a chance to play professionally because he had to work. The 1930s, of course, were the days of the Great Depression.

He did play semipro baseball and was very good. He was a pitcher and outfielder and played for one of the top teams in the nation, the old Eason Oilers. He also played for the Champlin Refineries, which won the national championship one year.

My father was not highly educated and worked for years as a truck driver for Failing Supply Company. But he had a heart as big as a house.

I remember having my nose pasted on a store window in Enid when I was about seven years old. I was looking at a first baseman's glove. It cost $9.10. It was a Lou Gehrig model. I knew I could never own it.

My dad went into the store and bought it. I bet it cost him a couple of meals a day for a month.

17

When I was a year old I accidentally burned my left leg with a hot iron. I've got a long scar and until I was fifteen I had a bit of a limp. I didn't have all of my calf. I really worked to develop it. In fact, I overworked it.

My dad liked to hunt and he would take me with him. We would walk as much as fifteen to twenty miles a day. With that walking and exercises, my burned leg developed so that now it's even bigger than my right one.

I grew up loving baseball. I started playing basketball in the seventh grade, mostly because I couldn't run very well and wanted to keep working on my leg.

I went out for the seventh grade basketball team and I got cut. I went out for the eighth grade team and got cut.

Then it became sort of an obsession with me. I was determined to learn to play basketball.

I was lucky in that I had a great coach at Longfellow Junior High. His name was Herbert Seem. He was very, very patient with me. He kept working with me and finally I got to play a little bit in the ninth grade.

All the time I was still playing baseball. It was American Legion ball.

The Legion games were in the evening. Afterwards, I would go over to nearby Phillips University, sneak in and play basketball until 11:30 or midnight. In the summer, I would work all day at a feed store. I would carry those big, heavy feed sacks on my shoulder and earn a dollar a day.

So there I was, working all day, playing baseball in the evening and shooting basketballs until late at night. My mother, Opal, would really get after me for going so hard. She could never figure where I would be next.

We had a great American Legion team. Our coach had pitched for the Brooklyn Dodgers many years before. He had a great curve ball and would teach us how to throw it and how to hit it.

I was pretty big by the time I was sixteen. I was six feet one and 160 pounds. I could hit the ball and pitch. I won over thirty American Legion games as a pitcher.

In high school, I lost one game and had a 9–1 record.

When I wasn't pitching I played the outfield.

We went to the state high school tournament my senior year. I pitched both games of a doubleheader in the regional play-offs and won both games. After that, a state rule was passed that no player could pitch within a space of a certain number of hours.

We went up against Capital Hills in the semifinals of the state tournament. One of their players was Tom Sturdivant, who later pitched for the New York Yankees.

Capital Hills was undefeated. I pitched and we beat them 1–0. Sturdivant got the only hit off me and I got the only two hits off him.

Because of the new rule, I couldn't pitch in the finals. We lost to Altus, Oklahoma.

I don't hold any grudge. It's a good rule because it protects young players.

I played some semipro ball after I got out of high school but my attention had turned more and more to basketball.

Three

ONE NIGHT the coach at Phillips University caught me in his gym at 11:30. I had broken in. He chased me all over the place and finally caught me. He got a board and busted me pretty good.

I was a freshman at Enid High School at the time. I couldn't shoot worth a lick. I couldn't even hit free throws. I tried every way I could think of. I'd shoot one-handed, two-handed and even underhanded.

But I had another patient coach. His name was Dale Holt. He's still one of my idols. He used to stay with me after regular practice and work with me. He'd stay as long as three hours.

He later told me something that meant more to me than anything else concerning basketball. He said I spent more time with basketball than anyone he'd seen.

I was one of the first players ever to shoot a jump shot. I'd shoot either off one foot or with both feet off the ground.

Coach Holt started me on that. I guess part of it was because of my leg.

My dad helped me a lot with my basketball, too. Like in baseball, he would play with me. He also made me a little bitsy basket, one like those you see in toy stores. He put it up in our backyard and I practiced a lot on it.

When I got to the gym, the basket there would look like a tub.

Nate Archibald, who played for me at Texas Western in the early 1970s, was a firm believer in those small baskets, by the way. He practiced on them, too.

How crazy was I about basketball? The night of the junior-senior prom, while people were dancing, I was shooting baskets.

There was a giant curtain at Convention Hall. On one side was the basketball court. On the other side was the dance floor. There I was shooting baskets by myself for three or four hours. I thought everybody on the other side of the curtain was nuts. I was perfectly content. I had no desire whatsoever to be on the other side of the curtain.

Our team went to the high school state tournament my sophomore and senior years.

I had made the team my sophomore year but I still wasn't very good. But I kept working at it. No one played basketball in the summer in those days, but I did. I played by myself, shooting and shooting.

We won a lot of games my junior and senior years. I became one of the leading scorers in the state but the scoring was much lower then.

One of the most memorable games came against Stillwater in the regional play-offs my senior year.

We started out the game with a zone and they started out with a man-to-man defense. Their coach told them to sit on the ball until we came out of the zone.

We got the tip and I took the first shot. I missed. It was the only shot taken the first half. They kept sitting on the ball, and I mean that literally. They would get the ball and sit down on the floor. Soon we joined them and there we were with both teams sitting on the floor as the clock ticked away.

Score at halftime was 0–0.

I took the first shot in the second half, too, and missed again.

Finally in the fourth quarter we came out of the zone and there was some scoring.

Near the end of the game the score was tied at 6–6. I got a rebound near the top of our circle and threw it, one-handed, nearly the length of the court. The ball went in the hoop, nearly tearing off the net.

We won 8–6.

The next day we all laughed about it. It was a freak shot, one you make maybe once in 50 tries. It even curved like a baseball.

It was no laughing matter for Stillwater, though. Their coach had a heart attack.

We advanced to the state tournament but lost there.

I received about a hundred scholarship offers from colleges.

My mother had cancer at the time and was very ill. A university (I'd rather not name it) offered me $3,300 for a cancer operation. The school would also pay me $100 a month. They told me all I had to do was "wind the clock."

My mother said I could go anywhere I wanted but that she would not accept the money for the operation. She also said she'd rather not have me get paid to wind a clock.

My dad agreed. The offer was turned down.

Another offer came from Phillips University. But I wasn't about to go there after the paddling I had taken from the coach.

Four

WHEN I ARRIVED at Oklahoma A&M as a freshman in 1949 I was a smart aleck. I'd been a big star in both baseball and basketball in high school and thought I knew it all. The next four years were to be a learning experience under coach Henry Iba.

I'd been a big fan of Oklahoma A&M for years and always wanted to play for Mr. Iba. I'd listen to their games every night they played when I was a kid. John Henry of radio station KVOO was a great announcer and I loved listening to him.

My high school coach didn't want me to go to Oklahoma A&M. He wanted me to go somewhere where I could shoot. I could shoot better than most people, thanks to all the practice I'd had. Mr. Iba didn't play that way, of course.

I had to learn a whole new way of life. In high school, if I missed five shots in a row Coach Holt would tell me not to worry, that I would make the next five. I never heard that at Oklahoma A&M.

I got chewed out for four years, which I needed. Mr. Iba told me one time, "You've been standing over there in the cool breeze shooting them long jump shots and them poor other guys are under the basket getting knots on their head."

But I'm getting ahead of my story.

I graduated from high school one night and the very next night I was out on the baseball diamond. There was a very good semi-pro team made up of college players, including Frank Kellert and others who later played in the majors. It was Class AA type baseball, at least.

I would get $350 a month.

I pitched all summer and did pretty well. But my future pitching career was stopped by a basketball injury.

The last day of basketball practice during my first year at Oklahoma A&M I was called in to work out with the basketball team. They had won the NCAA regionals and were fixing to play Kentucky.

I fell on my right elbow during the workout and hurt it pretty bad. They took me to the hospital and they wanted to operate. They told me I should never play any sports again because my arm would be crippled. They said I would have calcium in my elbow forever.

I didn't have the operation. My right arm is crooked even today.

My parents didn't try to talk me into quitting sports, though. They knew I'd never do it.

The injury ruined whatever career I might have had as a pitcher. It hurt when I shot basketballs the next year but I got over that.

I didn't give up baseball completely. I didn't play anymore college baseball but I remained on the semipro team and would play in the summers. I played third base and the outfield.

A year or two later I still couldn't pitch, but I tried. I couldn't throw hard but I learned how to throw a knuckleball. I was fairly successful but you can't do any good unless you can throw at least a little hard.

24

Five

I PLAYED THREE YEARS of varsity basketball at Oklahoma A&M. I started some games as a sophomore but I wasn't a great player. There's no doubt I could have done better at some other school but I have no regrets. I wouldn't have achieved what success I have as a coach if I hadn't gone there.

I consider Mr. Iba one of the greatest people in the world now, but I hated him then. All the players did.

Let me give you an example of how he worked. When I was a sophomore I made the All-College Tournament All-Star Team. That was quite an honor because that tournament brought together the eight best teams in the nation.

Mr. Iba benched me the next three games. That's the way he was. There were no individual stars on his teams.

The next game I started I missed my first five shots. I didn't even hit iron, I was so shook up.

I understand it now. Players can get cocky.

But I didn't understand that then. I would bitch and bitch. In fact, I was the clubhouse lawyer. I would get up on my soapbox and lead the complaining. I bitched all four years I was in college.

We players got along great. We were always so mad at Mr. Iba we didn't have time to bitch at each other.

25

Christmases were awful. During the two-week break we practiced three times a day, every day. The practices were from nine to twelve, two to five, and seven to ten. That was nine hours a day, and that included Christmas Day.

There were three times while I was there that we won games and then had chalk talk and practice afterwards. We had chalk talk from eleven to midnight then practiced until 5:00 A.M.

Mr. Iba used to tell an assistant coach that we were going out to shoot "a little" the day of a game. We knew what was coming. We'd run a play and Mr. Iba would get mad because it wasn't perfect. Then we'd stay for hours running over that play, and others.

We were in the finals of the All-College Tournament in Oklahoma City one day. We were to play at 7:30 that night. We went out at 1:00 P.M. "to shoot a little." At 5:00 P.M. we were still scrimmaging and they had to run us off the floor because there was a consolation game slated to start at that time. Mr. Iba was furious because they made us get off.

We won that night. We were afraid to lose.

It was like that all the time. We would show up at practice scared to death that someone would screw up because we knew we'd have to go over the play again and again. We couldn't leave the floor until we got it right.

We were scared of him away from the court, too. I'll never forget the night we were going to catch a train. There was a bus waiting on the campus. I, and a friend of mine, Bob Seymour, who was a super player, came out of a drugstore where we'd had a Coke and started walking toward the bus. Across the way we saw Keith Smith, a starter on our team, walking toward the bus holding hands with his girl friend.

And here comes the old green Oldsmobile with The Old

Man wearing his old brown suit and old brown hat. Mr. Iba didn't look either way but we knew he had seen us.

And Bob and I knew Smith had had it.

Smith's girl veered off and Smith got on the bus. Mr. Iba was waiting for him and chewed his butt for fifteen minutes.

Smith made the trip but he didn't play. Mr. Iba wasn't about to play anyone who didn't have his mind on basketball one hundred percent. Smith sat out all three games on the trip.

Mr. Iba also hated fraternities. He used to call them "lodges."

I agreed with him on that.

The fraternity guys really go after you, especially if you're an athlete. They talked me into joining one and I lasted one day. I quit when this guy told me to shine his shoes and that he was going to give me swats. I told him "adios."

Mr. Iba had a pipeline to everything. It was uncanny. He came up to me the next day and told me, "You went and joined one of those damn lodges, didn't you?" I was relieved that I was able to tell him I had quit.

I'll tell you how far his pipeline extended. I didn't drink beer at that time. There was a little bar near the campus called the Anchor Inn. I went in one day and got a Coke. I shouldn't have done it. Ten minutes later I was in his office.

One night some of our guys went to a party at a place called the Rock Inn. Mr. Iba found out about it and I still feel sorry for those guys. They went through hell for the next four days. It was inhumane, unbelievable. And all the guys involved were Army veterans. It didn't make any difference to Mr. Iba.

You didn't talk back to him. I tried one time. One time in four years. I said, "I thought . . ." That was as far as I got.

He told me I never had a damn thought in my life. Then he went into a ten-minute dissertation.

He'd dress you down in front of the whole team. But no one felt singled out. He did it to everybody. In fact, he'd single out one player at each workout. He'd get on his case from the word go. Everybody got his turn.

I don't hold anything against him for that. I've done it myself since I became a coach. Practice is like getting ready for war. You see what a guy can take. Usually, a guy who will crack in practice will crack on you in games.

One day it was my turn to be picked on. I happened to do everything right that day. I never went to a wrong spot. He came over to me, knowing I thought I had done everything right, and pointed to a board on the floor. "This board," he said, "this is the board you're supposed to go to, not that one." I was standing just inches away from the board he was pointing to.

He did smile at times. In fact, he had a good sense of humor. He would say some things in practice that would crack us up. Only thing, though, none of us dared laugh.

Six

I NEVER HAD MUCH foot speed. I could run pretty fast for a good distance but I didn't have those quick first and second steps like Bobby Joe Hill, our great guard in 1966.

I competed in track as a freshman. I ran a :49 in the 440 yard dash one time, which was pretty good then. And I high jumped, clearing six feet three, and broad jumped. My best broad jump was 23 feet 6 inches. I placed in some meets.

I also had a lot of stamina and because of that and my jumping ability I played the inside on our college basketball team.

We didn't lose a game my freshman year and we had hopes for the future. I started some games on the varsity my sophomore year. We won nineteen games and lost eight.

Mr. Iba was furious. A lot of teams would give anything to have a record like that but not Mr. Iba. He made us ashamed. We players went around the campus with our heads low.

We began working out in the summers as well as during the school term. I mean workouts with *him* out there. The rules were different then, of course. I'll never forget when the NCAA put a rule in that practice could not start until October 15. That was just before my senior year. We had a party to celebrate.

No one ever sat down during Mr. Iba's practices. And no one drank water. You might be out there for four hours but you never drank water.

I adopted that practice and didn't let my players at Texas Western College drink water during the 1960s. I do now, however. We had a reunion of our 1966 championship team in 1986 and they were all surprised to see our players drinking water during practice. "How come you're letting them drink water?" they asked me. "You never let us do it."

But getting back to Mr. Iba's practices, I'd get so cottonmouthed I'd get mad. I would threaten to quit. In fact, in my mind I quit every day for four years.

I'm sure the other players felt the same. But we stuck it out and must have developed because by the time I was a senior we were ranked No. 1 in the nation.

Two of the early games that stand out in my mind that senior year were against New Mexico A&M in Las Cruces. They were our second and third games of the season and we were heavily favored. The games had been scheduled because Mr. Iba was a good friend of the New Mexico A&M coach, who happened to be George McCarty. That's the same George McCarty who was later to be athletic director at Texas Western.

The reason McCarty and Mr. Iba got to be friends is that McCarty would come to Oklahoma A&M (which later changed its name to Oklahoma State just like New Mexico A&M changed its named to New Mexico State) to watch Iba's practices.

We players didn't take the games against New Mexico A&M very seriously. We had a great team and we knew it. New Mexico A&M's biggest player was a six feet two center. Our center was six feet eleven. His name was Bob Mattox and he was a whale of a player.

We won but New Mexico A&M played well and we didn't win by as big a margin as Mr. Iba thought we should have. Oh, he was mad.

After the games we drove back to Oklahoma. There was a long delay on the road near White Sands Missile Range. It seems a missile was to be fired and traffic was stopped. Cars were backed up a mile.

It was a policy of Mr. Iba's that after every game the team would stop and eat cereal and ice cream. We players hated it. We would rather have hamburgers and a Coke, but he thought the cereal and ice cream would be good for us.

We stopped at a restaurant but because of the delay on the road we couldn't get what Mr. Iba wanted. We were served hamburgers and French fries. Oh, we were delighted. But it only made Mr. Iba madder. Remember, he was already mad at us for not having played better against New Mexico A&M.

Mr. Iba didn't usually accompany us when we ate. He left that up to an assistant. But he was with us that night. He stood there watching us, one hand behind his back as he usually stood.

We players sat there perfectly quiet, not daring to say a word.

Then I made a mistake. I reached over, grabbed the ketchup bottle and poured some ketchup on my French fries.

He saw me and threw a fit. "What the hell do you want to do that for, Rope?" he growled. (He used to call me "Rope" because when my head got wet some strands of hair would come down over my forehead).

Mr. Iba was of the old school of coaching which thought things like ketchup were bad for your wind. I didn't think about that at the time, though.

I stopped with the French fry halfway to my mouth. I didn't know what to do for a moment. Then, with all the other players staring at me, I picked up my knife and scraped the ketchup off each French fry one by one.

Oh, it was embarrassing.

No one laughed, though. And Mr. Iba just kept standing there looking at me.

You notice I call him Mr. Iba. No one called him anything else. That was a tradition that was established before I got to Oklahoma A&M and one that continued after I left.

The waitress in the restaurant didn't know that, of course.

31

She kept calling him "Coach" and congratulating him on our victory. That made him angrier still.

Another incident I remember well was when we were playing for the conference championship in St. Louis. Bob Hendricks, a six feet six sophomore, was in the game. He was good but still a little inexperienced. With a few seconds to go, Mr. Iba called a play for us. I was supposed to throw the ball to Mattox. Hendricks, however, somehow got in front of him and I had to throw the ball to him. He went up and banged it against the glass backboard so hard he almost broke it. But the ball went in and we won.

Did I get thanks? No. After the game, Mr. Iba followed me all the way to the dressing room hollering such things as "you dumb dodo . . ." at me. Mr. Iba figured that Hendricks was a sophomore but that as a senior I should have known better.

The first black I played against was a fellow named Cleo Littleton. He played for Wichita University and he was really something. He was about six feet three. He had no calves in his legs but he could really jump.

Another black player I saw action against was K. C. Jones, who later became a star in the NBA and went on to coach the Boston Celtics.

Jones was with University of San Francisco. But that was before Bill Russell, and San Francisco didn't have that good a team when we went up against them. We beat them rather easily. Jones wasn't a very good shot but he was a heck of an athlete.

The rules were different then and Jones must have been with San Francisco some six years. He was still there when Russell led the Dons to the national championship.

We were ranked No. 1 going into the NCAA tournament

32

my senior year. No one on our team started every game, not even Mattox, who is the first big man I remember who could run and shoot like they do now. We had nine players who were about equal in ability and Mr. Iba would change starting lineups every game.

We should have won the national championship. We got beat by University of Kansas in triple overtime in Manhattan, Kansas.

We were way overconfident. We had played Kansas two weeks earlier and beaten them badly. It wasn't until the third overtime that the thought that we might get beat even entered my mind.

I had a hip pointer and didn't get to play much in that game. That hurt, but it hurts even more when I think the game was played on my birthday.

We finished with a 24–5 record.

Indiana won the national championship that year, beating Kansas by one point.

Seven

I MET MY WIFE, MARY, at Oklahoma A&M through another girl I had been dating. We were married my sophomore year.

It was not unusual then for sophomores to have wives. A

lot of the students were World War II veterans going to school on the GI Bill of Rights and were older than college kids are today. Although I wasn't a veteran, my wife and I lived in the same section of the campus as the veterans.

Like most college kids, we didn't have much money. We would sell Coke bottles to go to a movie. Mary would get mad at me because I collected dogs. I had all kinds of dogs. Hunting dogs, greyhounds, all sorts of strays. I had as many as eight dogs at one time. It cost money to feed them, of course, and that made Mary unhappy.

One day they broke into some cages where one of the other students kept rabbits and I had to pay for that, too.

While I was away on a trip, someone opened the kennel door and all my dogs escaped. To this day I suspect Mary was the culprit.

I finished the spring term in 1954 but I didn't graduate. I lacked some twelve hours. I did get a degree years later at West Texas State but not having one cost me a lot of money when I became a high school coach. That's why I've been so insistent that my players at University of Texas at El Paso graduate.

My first son, Mark, was born while I was still in college. My wife worked in the registrar's office and that helped us financially.

I went straight from college into AAU basketball. That's the Amateur Athletic Union. It was a big thing then. The NBA wasn't too popular yet and didn't pay well at all.

I had a chance to play with the Peoria Caterpillars but I turned it down. I didn't want to work with the Caterpillar company the rest of my life. I saw no future.

I got a call from G. C. "Red" Goodwin, coach of the Artesia [New Mexico] Travelers. They were a real good AAU team.

They played in the National Industrial Basketball League and paid very well — better than other teams in the league. I signed up.

I got the money to go to Artesia playing pool. I had played a lot when I was in high school and had gotten pretty good. I had a good friend in college by the name of Earl Estep. He's a dentist now in Athens, Texas. He, several others of our friends, and I won a couple of cars from a guy from Oklahoma City, playing pool. They were old cars but they were great for us college kids.

After my senior year, Estep and I got into a snooker game with a wheat farmer. Earl was great at hustling up games. We ended up winning $240. That helped me move my wife and son to Artesia.

Mary went to work at one of the Artesia banks.

The Travelers got me a job with rural electrification.

Slim Stewart, who became a lifelong friend, and several others on the team also worked for rural electrification. Most of us were "linemen." We were supposed to climb poles and fix wires. Most of us were screw-ups and didn't work very hard. We would just watch most of the time.

Not Stewart, who seemed to like to climb poles. I could climb up a little bit of the way. I think ten feet was my limit. And even then I would get splinters from my nose to my toes. Stewart got so good he could climb all the way up to the top of a ninety-foot pole.

We played a lot of games. My first visit to El Paso came on one of our road games, and it turned out to be a memorable one.

We played the Fort Bliss team, which was made up of soldiers. A lot of their players were former college stars.

Some of us on the Artesia team, making our first trip to

the border, were more interested in visiting Juarez, but the game turned out to be a donnybrook.

There was a player on the Fort Bliss team who was from some place in the East. Maybe Brooklyn. I could tell by his accent. The guy talked all the time we were playing. On one play he kicked my instep and I fell. I skinned my knee pretty good. The guy who tripped me told me I was clumsy.

When we got to the middle of the floor again he tripped me again.

Our team had a big post man, about six feet eleven. His name was Don Holt. I moved him out of the middle. I caught the ball with one hand and swung my other arm backwards. I knew the guy who had tripped me was right behind me.

I caught him with my elbow and knocked seven or eight of his teeth out.

I thought for sure there would be a riot. The place was full of soldiers.

My elbow was bleeding. I went over to our bench and sat down. I thought I was going to be thrown out of the game.

There was a black official working the game. He came over and asked Coach Goodwin if he had taken me out. Goodwin said, "No. Didn't you kick him out?"

"No," the official said, "I called a jump ball."

He told us later that the fellow who had tripped me had been doing things like that all year.

I played for Artesia for a couple of years. Our road trips would consist of as many as twenty-seven games.

McCarty later coached Texas Western and I played with Artesia against his team. We played the game at El Paso Coliseum. The Miners had fine players like Alvis Glidewell and Ed Haller, who later became coaches, and darn good ones.

I don't know if McCarty had anything to do with helping them become coaches but I know he influenced me. After that game at the Coliseum he took me over to a little room and talked to me. He said, "Why don't you get into coaching?"

I told him I really didn't want to, that I wasn't really interested. But he set me to thinking. Here I was about twenty-four years old and I still didn't know what I was going to become. You can't play basketball forever.

I had played against a fellow named Fordy Anderson while in college. He later became the basketball coach at Bradley University. He was a fine coach. My college team played against him and we always had a difficult time because his teams could play slow or play fast.

Later in the year after we had played Texas Western and McCarty had talked to me I decided to attend the New Mexico Coaches Clinic in Albuquerque. Anderson and McCarty were both there. I don't know exactly why I went. I was still debating my future and I guess I went to find out some more about coaching.

I went to the restaurant of the old Sunset Inn. McCarty was sitting with Polk Robinson, athletic director at Texas Tech. McCarty offered me a chance to come to Texas Western as a graduate assistant, which would give me the opportunity to get my degree.

If I'd known then what I know now I would have taken the job. Instead, I told him no thanks, that if I were to coach it would have to be as a head coach somewhere.

Robinson heard me. He got up and went to a nearby telephone and called a man who had called him from Benjamin, Texas, looking for a coach. Robinson motioned me over and I talked to the man on the other end of the line. It was D. V.

Markham, superintendent of schools and a former football star at Hardin-Simmons University. He offered me the job despite learning I didn't have a degree. He told me I would have to coach football, boys basketball, girls basketball and drive the bus.

I didn't know what I was getting into but I accepted anyway.

Eight

BENJAMIN WAS A TOWN of about three hundred people. There was only one stop light in the whole town. And only one restaurant.

The facilities at the stadium were terrible. Broken glass on the field, that type of thing. And the house we were to live in came as quite a shock when we first drove up and saw it. The house was small but really not all that bad. But the yard was full of weeds — and there was a huge rattlesnake in them!

I know Mary was scared to death, and I thought to myself, "What am I doing here?" It was tough, yet Mary never complained, never nagged.

But the people in Benjamin were real friendly and that sure helped.

My driving job paid $400 a year, which brought my annual salary to $3,200. I would have gotten more if I'd had a degree. I'd get up real early to drive the bus. It was about an hour-and-a-half run. Mary would drive it now and then when I couldn't.

I didn't know how to coach football, and I was sort of scared. But I wasn't going to let anybody know it. I acted real tough, just like I had learned from Mr. Iba, and hollered at the kids a lot. A person goes back to what he has learned.

It was six-man football and we had only nine boys out for the team. Mr. Markham helped me a lot, thank goodness. He would show me what a cross-block was, things like that. He probably did as much coaching as I did.

The players responded. We wound up winning the district football championship, which was the first time Benjamin had ever won it.

My wife and I got to be friends with some of the families. One of them was the Hudson family. Their son, Johnny, was on our football team. One day Mary and I were invited to a get-together at the McFadden Ranch, where Johnny's father was foreman. It was a huge ranch and the scene was just like an old western roundup. The cowboys had chaps on like in the movies and sat around a fire drinking coffee.

Our team had lost the bi-district game (my biggest game as a coach up to that time) that week and I was down in the dumps. The cowboys, who had been to the game, tried to cheer me up. They suggested I go horseback riding. I'd never done much riding and I wasn't up to it anyway. But they kept insisting and got me on a horse called Old Lightning. He was red and had bloodshot eyes.

As soon as I got on him, one of the cowboys hit him. That sucker took off across the prairie. I didn't know how to ride so I dropped the reins and grabbed the saddle horn.

The horse was going too fast for me to jump off, and I had to stay on until he ran out of gas.

The cowboys laughed and laughed and called me "cowboy." When I got off I went chasing after them but couldn't catch any of them.

But you know what? It took my mind off the game we'd lost and made me realize there are more important things in life.

Another incident I remember while at Benjamin came at Christmas time. Mary went to Oklahoma to visit her parents. I drove her there and on the way back I stopped in Wichita Falls for a beer. I hadn't had one in months. You just didn't drink in Benjamin.

There was a snooker table in the place I went into and there were a couple of guys playing. I sat down to drink my beer and watched.

One of the players, after finishing a game, turned to me and said, "Hey, buddy, you want to play?" I told him I'd love to.

He started hustling me. He asked me if I would like to play for a beer. "Sure," I said. Then he asked me if I'd like to play for a dollar instead. I said, "Okay." Then he upped it to two dollars. I only had ten dollars in my pocket but I accepted.

I won. He doubled up. I won again. We finally wound up playing for a hundred dollars. I quit fooling around and was very careful on my shots. That was a lot of money then.

After I'd won, I reached over for the money. He grabbed my hand. "What would you say if I didn't pay you," he said.

"Get your damn hand off mine," I told him.

Then he pulled back his coat and showed me a deputy

40

sheriff's badge. Immediately I thought, "I can't get into trouble. I'm a coach and a school teacher." I backed off.

One fellow started cussing him, and he and other patrons in the bar followed him to his car cussing him out. The bartender had told him to get out.

All that was fine, but I never got my hundred bucks.

We had pretty good basketball success at Benjamin, too. Remember, I was coaching both boys and girls. I took both teams to a tournament in a nearby town. The boys got beat 30–29 by Noodle, Texas. The girls lost by a point, too.

I drove the bus there and back. After we got back I worked the teams until 3:00 A.M.

I treated the girls just as tough as I did the boys. I had the boys working on one end of the floor and the girls on the other and I'd go down and cuss the girls a while then go over to the boys and cuss them a while.

I got only about an hour's sleep that night. I had to get up early to drive the bus.

There were some disgruntled people after that. One lady on the school board went after my scalp. But although I'd been very hard on the players, they came to my defense.

A little later we went to a tournament in Hedley, Texas. There was a man there who got the entire Hedley school board to come and talk to me.

They offered me the job there and I took it. It was a "big jump." I went from a town of three hundred to a town of five hundred.

What happened next was ironic. The man who had gotten the Hedley school board together to talk to me had a son named Bill Reeves. He was a fine player and was going to be on the Hedley team. His parents were both killed in an auto accident even before I took the job.

41

Bill wound up going to Plainview High School instead of Hedley. Both Benjamin and Hedley were Class B schools; Plainview was Class AAAA. Bill became a fine college player and then became athletic director at University of Texas at Arlington.

Basketball had been down at Hedley before I got there and the loss of Bill Reeves didn't help. But we went to work. We had to hold our basketball workouts at night because many of the players picked cotton and did other farm work during the day. The Texas Interscholastic League hadn't put in any rules limiting practice yet so we used to practice basketball year-round.

In a couple of years, we became the team to beat in our district. I had a player by the name of Bobby Roland. He couldn't walk and chew gum when he was in the eighth grade. But he was a hard worker. It took me months to teach him how to jump off his left foot and shoot with his right hand. But he became my pride and joy. He later went to West Texas State then to Texas Western. He was never a great college player but what he achieved with what he had to work with was tremendous.

I was coaching the girls team, too, just like I did at Benjamin. And like I say, I treated the girls just as rough as I did the boys. Or I thought I did. Luckily, I didn't have to coach football.

I got to meet a fellow who became a lifelong friend. His name is Jim Evans. He lived up the street from where we moved in.

I set a state record for technical fouls in one of our girls games. I was trying to intimidate the referee and I walked out on the floor. He gave me a technical for every step I took. Sixteen steps, sixteen technicals.

42

I was so hard on the girls I figured they'd never forget me. During one game, one of our girls, Jeannie Sanders, dived for a ball and was slow getting up. I bawled her out good.

When I got home I was informed that girls have "periods." I didn't think about that. No girl ever told me she couldn't play because she was in that condition.

Maybe I eased up a little after that. One day we were in the finals of a tournament with both the boys and girls teams. The girls played first and won. They came over to wish me luck. One of the girls said I was favoring the boys because I was tougher on them than I was on the girls.

I also had complaints from some of the girls' mothers. They told me they wanted their girls chewed out just like the boys.

Coaching girls showed me something about women. I don't remember a girl ever quitting, but I've had boys quit.

After I'd been at Hedley a couple of years I heard from my players about a boy on the Borger High School B team by the name of Bobby Lesley. The boys said he could really play.

I went over and saw him. I'll never forget the first time I set eyes on him. He was barefooted, freckle-faced and hard as a rock. He was cocky, too, but could he play. And he was a good student to boot.

I talked to his mother. They had lived in Hedley before they moved to Borger.

The only way we could get Bobby from Borger to Hedley was if he had a legal guardian. I got him one. Me.

He stayed at Hedley with Sue and O'Neill Weatherly. The Weatherlys were really good to him.

Lesley, despite being cocky, was really a good kid. He didn't have any bad habits.

He led us to the semi-finals of the state tournament one year. It was the first time Hedley had ever advanced that far.

We got a lot of writeups. Some of them were by Eddie Mullens and Putt Powell of the *Amarillo Globe-News*. I got to be friends with Eddie and later when I was at Texas Western, I recommended him for the job of sports information director. He got the job and was with us when we won the national championship in 1966. And we are still together with the Miners more than twenty years later.

While at the regional meet with Hedley, I ran into George McCarty again. He had resigned as basketball coach at Texas Western and wanted me to apply for the job. He never gave up. I have to give him credit. Here I was coaching a Class B high school team and he was offering me a head coaching job at a major college.

He tried hard to get me the job but I didn't get it. Harold Davis was hired.

McCarty told me, "I'm going to get you out our way some day."

Nine

MY FOUR YEARS AT HEDLEY were a lot of fun. And we had the rest of my four boys while I was there. I also attended West Texas State and got my college degree.

But I was getting anxious to move up. I looked around for some higher classification schools. I went to Amarillo to see if I could get the basketball job there. The position had become open. Mullens and Powell had written so many good things about me that I figured I had a good chance at getting the job. But I was turned down. They told me I didn't have enough experience.

I went to Big Spring, Texas next. Texas, as everybody knows, has always been a football state, especially on the high school level. It was a long drive in my old car and I rehearsed my presentation on the way. I sat down and gave the athletic director my long spiel. It turned out the athletic director was also the football coach. "I don't want a basketball coach who's going to try that hard," he told me.

Boy, was I disillusioned.

But I kept making applications. I applied even at New Mexico schools like Belen and Truth or Consequences.

Meanwhile, the boys basketball position at Dumas, Texas opened up. The coach there was Rex Fox, who became a good friend of mine. He was a very intelligent man and a great teacher. He taught algebra and other subjects in addition to coaching. Ironically, he left Dumas to become a professor at Texas Western. He's still there.

I applied. The Dumas school board was split on whom to hire. Basketball coaching jobs were usually filled by assistant football coaches in Texas then. Bill Spann, one of the assistant football coaches, had applied too.

I got the job because of J. R. Yell, a very tough individual who happened to be on the school board. He was in my corner and really helped me.

I was lucky that Mr. Yell and others who voted for me wanted a basketball coach who didn't have to help with football, too, and wanted to upgrade the basketball program.

45

Burl Bartlett was head football coach. Spann became my assistant.

Incidentally, Fox had been not only a good basketball coach who left the program in good shape, but he had been assistant football coach, too. And he had done a good job in football, as well.

It was a bit touchy having Spann as my assistant because he had been an applicant for the job. But we got along well. In fact, we all got along. I've always considered it a bit silly for coaches at the same school having problems. We all have a job to do and it's better to be working together than against each other.

Things worked out well in the end. The next year, Bartlett left to become an assistant football coach at Texas Tech and Spann became the head football coach at Dumas. I know Spann was more of a football man than a basketball man so he was happy.

I was at Dumas just one year and it was a good one. We won the district, bi-district and regional titles. Some of the players on the team went on to good college careers. One was Kelly Baker, who was six feet six and became a fine player at University of Texas at Austin. Another was Larry Tyner, who later played with Rice. Still another was Jimmy Morgan, who played with Abilene Christian.

Not only were they good athletes, all of them were members of the National Honor Society.

George McCarty was on the phone again that summer. By now he was dean of men at Texas Western. He told me to come down for an interview. Harold Davis had resigned and was going into private business.

Ten

I DROVE TO EL PASO from Dumas in a brand new station wagon they had given me at Dumas. I guess a lot of coaches have done that. They get rewards for being successful then they move on.

I arrived in El Paso and stayed at La Posta Motor Lodge which is located near the college. Frankly, I was scared to death.

The first person I was introduced to is one of the finest persons I've ever met, Ben Collins. He was head football coach and athletic director. He had only two assistants, Jimmy Walker and Ken George, and both taught a full load. Still, Ben did a good job. There were many years after him that the school didn't win as many games as when he was coach.

Collins and McCarty took me to meet Dr. Joseph Ray, the president of the school.

Dr. Ray sat there smoking his pipe and asking questions. I really wasn't questioned that much on my basketball. Dr. Ray wanted to know if I could take care of the dorm. It seems they had been having a lot of problems there.

Don't get me wrong. I'm not saying he wasn't interested in my coaching. He said McCarty had already convinced him that I could coach.

47

Later a joke was made of the interview. It was said that I wasn't hired because I could coach but because I was tough enough to take care of the dorm.

But it wasn't that way at all. Dr. Ray put both McCarty and Collins on the spot. He turned to Collins and asked him if I was the man he really wanted. "He's coming from a little school," he told Collins, "are you willing to take responsibility?"

Ben said, "Yes, I am."

So I'll always be grateful to both McCarty and Collins. I don't know if I would have done the same. My background was really weak when you think about it. I'd been successful but it was at small schools.

I kept in constant touch with McCarty and Collins for a month-and-a-half after the interview. I worried all the time. I was sure something had gone wrong. McCarty had told me it was just a matter of formality but I thought for sure it was going to fall through.

One of the other persons being considered seriously for the job was Tom Chavez, who was doing an outstanding job at Jefferson High School in El Paso. Had he been chosen he would have done very well. I was really impressed watching his teams play. In fact, I would go over and watch his practices. He had been coach of the Mexican Olympic team. He used a 1–3–1 offense which I thought was real good.

I finally got the call that I had been hired by Texas Western. The year was 1961. I loaded up my station wagon and rented a U-Haul. I piled my wife and four boys (Mark, Brent, Steve and David) in and we took off. By the way, the full name of my second son is Brent Dale Haskins. The "Dale" is for my high school coach, Dale Holt.

I took a pay cut. The job at Texas Western paid $6,500. I

got $9,000 a year at Dumas. But there were extras. We lived in an apartment in Miner Hall and ate there, all free.

But money was really immaterial. I came to Texas Western for the opportunity. I would have come for free.

I had quite an introduction to the El Paso Southwest. The day in August I was due to arrive in El Paso was the day of the first airplane hijacking. It happened at El Paso International Airport. The story was being reported on the radio. We first heard it when we were near Alamogordo, New Mexico. The airplane's tires had been shot out and there was a lot of excitement.

I guess I was paying more attention to the radio than my driving because I was pulled over for speeding. I was taken to a little town named Orogrande. The judge was the owner of the service station. He took off his Texaco cap and tried me on the spot. He lectured me and fined me $45.

I barely had enough money.

Eleven

THE FIRST PLAYER I MET at Texas Western was Nolan Richardson. He was standing in front of the dorm when I pulled up with my U-Haul and he helped me unload.

Richardson had been a great athlete at Bowie High School in El Paso. He starred in football, baseball and, of course, basketball. He and some other players had already been recruited.

I would say Richardson has come a long way since he helped me unload my U-Haul. He became head basketball coach at University of Tulsa, then University of Arkansas.

Not long after we got settled down I got a call from Bobby Lesley. He had signed a letter to go to Rice and was working in the oil fields in Odessa, Texas during the summer.

He came down for a visit. He was a mess when he arrived. He had been driving all night and had on an old dirty shirt and was barefooted.

Collins happened to see him. He didn't say anything at the time but a day or two later he pulled me aside and said, "Uh, Don, you may not know this, but you may not win many games if you bring in a bunch of guys from Hedley."

I guess he thought all the players from Hedley looked like Lesley and that was the way they dressed.

Letters of intent weren't binding in those days like they are now. They weren't even nationally recognized. I signed Lesley.

And Collins became one of his biggest fans. Oh, Collins came to love him.

Lesley was the first player I recruited. The second was Bobby Joe Hill. But it wasn't the Bobby Joe Hill who helped us win the national championship. They had exactly the same name but they weren't related.

My third recruit was Willie Brown, who played for a junior college in New York. Harold Davis had contacted him but hadn't signed him.

Brown would write to me every day. I mean *every day*. He wanted to come west in the worst way.

He wrote so much I decided he couldn't play. But he

impressed my wife, who was the first to go through our mail. She kept telling me to bring him down. She never interferes with my recruiting but he had really got to her.

I finally sent for him. He came down on an airplane and I went to pick him up. He was sporting a great, big mustache. My first words to him were, "Take that damn thing off."

He did. The next day after I watched him practice I was so impressed I went over, put my arm around him and told him he could grow a mustache back but to make it smaller.

Frankly, I didn't know a thing about college rules when I took over the job in August. I started working out the players right away. And I mean I worked them hard. I had four players leave even before school started, and I wasn't even supposed to be practicing.

The schedule had been set already, of course. Our first three games were whoppers. They were against Iowa State, Tulsa and Oklahoma State — all on the road.

On the way to our first game we stopped in Lubbock, Texas and scrimmaged Texas Tech. They had a good team and beat us pretty bad.

I worked my guys until five in the morning. It was unbelievable how hard I worked them. It was unmerciful.

But by the time their first game came around they were ready.

Before we left El Paso, Dr. Ray came into where we were eating breakfast. We were awfully impressed. It was real early in the morning, about five A.M., and here was the president of the college wishing us luck.

Iowa State had a great player named Venny Brewer. He was about six feet seven.

The sports writers in Iowa had given the school hell for playing such a small school, just like sports writers in El

Paso have given me hell for scheduling teams like Appalachian State, Arlington, New Mexico Highlands and so on.

Players read the papers, and I could see the Iowa players looking us over as we warmed up. I could see the lack of respect in their eyes.

But all the work we'd done and the support we'd had from people like Dr. Ray paid off. We upset Iowa State 66–59.

Brewer played great, but we had an all-around well-balanced team.

Besides the players I've mentioned we had top notch players like Gordon Taylor, Danny Vaughn, Paul Hines, Jerry Ray, Ted Sterrett.

We were small but athletic. Richardson could play like he was six feet seven and Hill played like he was a seven footer. Hill was a real leaper, and all our guys could shoot.

We lost to Tulsa 76–66 and Oklahoma State 63–57. They were close games, especially considering they were on the road.

We were in the Border Conference that year. It was tough. Both Arizona and Arizona State were in it.

Arizona State wound up as champion after beating us in two close games.

We finished my first season at Texas Western with an 18–6 won-lost record.

Twelve

TEXAS WESTERN DROPPED OUT of the Border Conference the following year and went independent.

It was a strange year, but I had picked up a great player and I could see the makings of a really outstanding team. His name was Jim Barnes. Mullens, who liked to put nicknames on all our players, called him "Bad News" Barnes because he was exactly that to the opposition.

I first heard of Barnes from Gerald Stockton, a college teammate of mine who was coaching Barnes at Cameron Junior College in Oklahoma. Stockton later became head basketball coach at Midwestern College.

Stockton not only told me about Barnes, he told me exactly what to do to get him. Barnes was being recruited by a lot of schools and was being offered all kinds of things.

Gerald talked to him like a father. He told him not to take anything from any school, that it was illegal. Heck, I couldn't offer him anything if it was legal. My entire recruiting budget for the year then was $5,000 and I used up most of it driving back and forth to Oklahoma trying to get him.

Barnes was having a hard time making up his mind. One day he was shooting free throws in his junior college gym. I walked up to him, put the signing papers on the free throw line and challenged him to a free throw contest in front of his teammates. I told him that if I beat him he would come to Texas Western. If I lost, I would leave him alone.

He accepted.

We decided the contest would consist of twenty-five free throws. The one who made the most out of twenty-five would be the winner.

I shot first and made all twenty-five of my shots.

Barnes missed on his second and third tries, and he was mine.

He was six feet seven.

Cameron JC had recruited him out of Arkansas while he was still in high school. His whole family moved to Stillwater, Olkahoma with him. With Barnes on the team, Stillwater High School went 20–0. Then some stuff came out before the play-offs about how he was recruited and he was made ineligible for a whole year. Stillwater had three other blue chip players who later played major college basketball and Stillwater went on to win the state tournament. With Barnes, it would have been even easier.

The next year, with the other blue chippers gone and Barnes on the sidelines, Stillwater had a terrible regular season. It went something like 3–20. Barnes became eligible at play-off time and he led Stillwater, horrible record and all, to the state championship!

He was that great.

Incidentally, one of Barnes' best friends was a guy by the name of Ulysses Kendall. He was a topnotch football player at Cameron and was being highly recruited, too. Bum Phillips, later of pro football fame, had become head football coach at Texas Western and I brought Kendall back with me. I'm sure Phillips appreciated it. Kendall not only did a fine job at Texas Western but went on to play with the Philadelphia Eagles.

Barnes had an old car which was held together by baling wire. It was awful.

I followed him to El Paso because I was afraid that old clunker of his would break down before he got there. Sure enough, it did. The carburetor gave out in Benjamin, Texas of all places. That's where I had my first coaching job.

I knew a mechanic there and he took the car to his garage and fixed it. It cost $20.

When we finally got to El Paso I got Barnes a job at American Smelter and Refining Company (ASARCO). He made $1.96 an hour, which seemed like pretty good money then.

Barnes traded in his old car for a 1954 Dodge. It wasn't much, but it was better than that old wreck he had.

He showed me two letters he had received while he was being recruited by colleges. One offered him a brand new Impala. The other told him he wouldn't have to attend class. Of course, both offers were illegal. The latter, by the way, was written by a professional player who had attended the college making the offer. The writer told Barnes he had taken a pay cut to turn pro.

A lot of people around the Southwest — and around the country — were wondering how I got Barnes to come to Texas Western. Who would believe I got him in a free throw shooting contest?

Barnes hadn't been in El Paso more than a week or so when Dr. Ray called me in. The president of a nearby university told him that Barnes was driving around in a Cadillac. Dr. Ray, of course, had to check it out.

I said, "Really, Dr. Ray, that's not true."

Just then Barnes drove up. I was standing up in Dr. Ray's

office and happened to look out the window. I motioned to Dr. Ray to come take a look.

He saw Barnes get out of his 1954 Dodge. I said, "Dr. Ray, there's that Cadillac." He laughed.

George McCarty got on me, too, about that time but for a different reason. He said I shouldn't have spent nearly all my recruiting budget on one player.

It was a gamble, all right. I had put all my marbles in one basket.

But it was a gamble that would pay off.

Thirteen

COACH STOCKTON HAD TOLD ME Barnes wouldn't be easy to coach, that he wouldn't always show up for practice.

But I tried to treat him like all the other players. One day he showed up for practice fifteen minutes late. I ran him up and down the stairs one entire day. I thought he was going to go home. He pouted and sulked but he didn't quit.

I had told him he could do for Texas Western what Elgin Baylor had done for Seattle. Seattle had been nothing until Baylor got there then suddenly it was a powerhouse.

I was right. Barnes' first season with us (1962–63) we won nineteen games and lost only seven. In his senior year, the 1963–64 season, we went 25–3 and nearly won the national championship. In fact, we should have won it. The only three games we lost were the ones in which Barnes fouled out.

He was just a natural all-around athlete. He could jump and shoot and was quick as a cat despite his size. If he had one fault, it was that he was too unselfish. He averaged twenty-nine points his senior year and didn't put the ball up that much. The most shots he ever put up were against Texas A&M in the NCAA play-offs in our 25–3 year. He hit on twenty-three of twenty-six field goal tries and set a Field House record. We won 68–62 and it wasn't that close.

He set all kinds of school records at Texas Western and many of them still stood more than twenty-five years later. They include most points scored in a game — 51; highest scoring average for a season — 29.2; most free throws attempted in a season — 295; most free throws made in a season — 210; most rebounds in a season — 537; most field goals made in a season — 299. All those were set his senior year.

He holds all-time career school records in scoring average — 24.0; highest field goal percentage — .532; best rebound average — 17.9; and most rebounds — 965.

After beating Texas A&M in the regionals, we went up against Kansas State. Barnes played a total of eight minutes and we lost 64–60.

I still have a bad taste in my mouth about that game. He was charged with four quick touch fouls. It really bothered me and since watching the film afterwards, I've always been suspicious of those fouls.

Even so, we almost beat Kansas State. And we would have if our first Bobby Joe Hill had stayed eligible. He had flunked out at midterm.

Kansas State lost to UCLA by a point in the finals.

We had some real gutty players on that team. One was Steve Tredennick. I admired him a lot. I had recruited him from Burges High in El Paso. He had averaged something like twenty-five points a game in high school but he was a step slow. He was as hard-nosed as they come and one of our best defensive guards. Talk about a no-quit guy. I used to work him out real hard and sort of hoped he would quit. I thought he needed to quit.

But he didn't know the meaning of the word. He went on and became a great lawyer after graduation. He probably wouldn't have become that if he'd quit in basketball. Athletics really do tell what kind of person one is.

Another gutty guy on the team was Bobby Dibler who became one of the best basketball officials in the country.

He wasn't very big. I recruited him from Amarillo Junior College. He was lefthanded and a cocky little devil. He really helped our team attitude.

Others on the team included Harry Flournoy and Orsten Artis. Those two were to help us win the national championship a couple of years later but they were sophomores at the time.

Waiting in the wings were David Lattin, Willie Cager and the second Bobby Joe Hill. They had already been recruited and were being red-shirted [held out a year]. They, too, would help us win the national title in 1966.

Fourteen

THE 1964–65 SEASON was a floundering one. We would go like a ball of fire then play real crummy.

Barnes was gone and we had no real post man. We used Nevil Shed there but he was really a forward and wasn't that big. The second Bobby Joe Hill was on the team and that helped. We finished with sixteen wins but nine losses.

We did get invited to the National Invitation Tournament. We lost to Manhattan in the first game 71–54. Shed came down with a hip pointer before the game and couldn't play. That really hurt us. I tried Flournoy at the post but he was new to it and he was only six feet five.

We were really better than the score against Manhattan indicates. The only place they could beat us that bad was in Madison Square Garden where the tournament was held. It's just a tough place to beat an eastern team.

I learned a lot during that '64–'65 season.

We had guys who would show up late and if it wasn't one thing going wrong it was another. And I used poor judgment in many cases.

I sat Bobby Joe out two games. I had told him to get me a card with his grades. I knew he wasn't going to do it. It wasn't that he was disobedient or defiant. It's just that Bobby Joe was easy going and his mind was here one moment and there the next.

59

He was a good kid but I trapped myself. I told him I would sit him out if he didn't get me the card and when he didn't get it to me I did.

Then I set a rule down that the next guy who would be late for a pregame meal would be kicked off the team. And guess who it was? The guy who never did anything wrong, Jimmy Holmes.

We were eating and here comes Jimmy. He had a legitimate excuse. He had been in class.

I feel bad about it even today. He was a good kid from El Paso who was trying real hard.

I had to kick him off the team because I said I would. I had put myself in a box.

To this day, I consider that my worst case of poor judgment.

George McCarty had warned me not to do such things. You don't do anybody any good by putting somebody off the team. Like McCarty said, what do you prove? You just hurt the player and the team. The only time you kick someone off the team is if he does something really terrible.

I'm sure Jimmy feels bad towards me to this day, and he ought to. You know what he became after graduation? You know what a solid citizen he is?

He became a judge.

Willie Cager was an unusual recruiting case. He didn't go to high school so he never played at that level. He got his high school diploma by going to night school.

Dr. J. M. Whitaker, then superintendent of El Paso Public Schools, was a big help. He would counsel players and help them any way he could.

Another Willie, Willie Brown, my former player, had told me about Nevil Shed who was going to North Carolina A&T. And he mentioned Cager, too.

I never saw Shed nor Cager play before they arrived at Texas Western. But Brown had seen them and I took his word that they could play. And he was right.

Brown, by the way, became a vice president with E. F. Hutton. This was the fellow I had told to shave off his mustache.

Another person who helped me recruit some of our key players that year was Hilton White, who ran a playground in New York. He coached a lot of teams and saw a lot of good players. I came to know him through Willie Brown.

White had been in El Paso while in the service. He told me he would help me get players on one condition: That I would make sure they got help if needed to get a good education.

He recommended Willie Worsley, who was small but turned out to be a great asset to our title team.

White recommended another small player who weighed only 125 pounds but, he said, was a great player.

I told him, "Come on, I don't want a player who only weighs 125 pounds."

He kept insisting, telling me I had to take him. He finally said that if I didn't take this player he would never recommend anybody to me again.

I said I would take a look at him when I got a chance.

The player's name was Nate Archibald.

Fifteen

IT WAS OBVIOUS that we would need a big man for our 1965–66 season, and I was lucky I had him.

I had scouted David Lattin at the Texas High School Tournament a couple of years before. He completely dominated the tournament and led his team, Worthing High School of Houston, to the championship. I tried real hard to recruit him. I don't know how many trips I made to Houston and I called him on the telephone so often I still remember his telephone number more than twenty years later.

He would have come to Texas Western right out of high school but I couldn't meet his demands. I had told him about all the records Jim Barnes had set and he was so confident he told me he wanted to break them.

But he told me he would come only if I took four of his buddies on the Worthing High School team. "Coach," he said, "take these other cats and I'll come."

The four couldn't play a lick. I told him, "No, David."

So he and these other four "cats" went to Tennessee A&I.

I guess he didn't like it. The school didn't play much of a schedule. After he'd been there about a semester he called me about three in the morning one day. He said, "Coach, this is Dave."

I was half asleep. "Dave who?" I asked.

"David Lattin," he replied. "Coach, if you send me a plane ticket I'll come on down to Texas Western."

I said, "David, I can't do that. It's illegal."

That really hurt me. If ever I thought of doing something against NCAA rules it was then. I thought about it all day. "Jesus," I said to myself, "what's a little old plane ticket?"

But I just couldn't bring myself to do it.

I did tell David that if he could find his way to El Paso I'd take him.

The next morning, my phone rings at 5:00 A.M. I'm half asleep again.

"Coach, this is Dave again," I heard on the phone.

I said, "Now, Dave, just get on down here."

He said, "Coach, I'm here. I came in on the bus."

Boy, I got dressed in a hurry and ran down to the Greyhound station to pick him up.

Sometimes you don't know your players as well as you think you do. Dave was so big and tough I thought I'd have trouble with him. I thought he would be a drinker and a hell-raiser.

He never smoked and he never drank. And he still doesn't. He once told me the only bad habit he had was "chasing babes."

It wasn't that he was particularly religious or anything, he just liked to take care of himself. We had our twenty-year reunion in 1986 and he looked in great physical condition. He plays tennis and I bet he could still play a good brand of basketball.

Sixteen

RECRUITING OF BLACKS wasn't widespread in the country when I was hired at Texas Western. But El Paso is a unique place and there was no problem in that respect. El Paso has a large Hispanic population and acceptance of different cultures had long been established. Blacks have not encountered animosity like in some other cities.

When I took the job at Texas Western in 1961 there were already blacks on the team. Charlie Brown was the first of that color to play for the Miners.

Nolan Richardson was already on the team when I got there, and Harold Davis had already recruited Willie Brown. The first black I recruited was the first Bobby Joe Hill.

I got the second Bobby Joe Hill from Burlington Junior College in Iowa. I red-shirted him the first year.

I'm color blind when it comes to recruiting. I look for players, period. If I wanted a perfect racial balance I could go out and get me as many white, black or Hispanic players as I wanted. But that's not the way I work. I don't recruit anyone just to sit on the bench.

I look for players according to position. I try to get the best man possible for a certain position. Size isn't a sole consideration. People are always talking about seven-footers. I could go out and get some but most of them can't play.

I'd like to have six-four guards, if they could play. The ones who can usually go to bigger schools.

Our 1965–66 team is a good example of what I look for. Everyone could play. When our rebounding developed as the season progressed I figured we had a good team. We wound up as the leading rebounding team in the nation. It's usually the top rebounding teams that go far in the play-offs.

We had guys who could play great defense, too. Bobby Joe Hill and Orsten Artis were tops in that department. Hill was more exciting because he stole balls but Orsten was probably sounder and was not only a great individual defensive player but an outstanding team defensive player.

In the middle we had Lattin. He was a force and could do everything. He was a first-round NBA choice the next year. At six-six there aren't many players who can play center but he could. He totally dominated a game.

On one wing we had Harry Flournoy, who wasn't a great shooter but was our leading rebounder. I've never had a better rebounder.

Then there was Nevil Shed, who was a great player, and Willie Worsley, who was small but could do a lot of things, and Willie Cager, who could also do a lot of different things.

Others on the team, none of them black, were Jerry Armstrong, Dick Myers, David Palacio, Togo Railey and Louis Baudoin.

We had different type players and they molded into champions.

I first learned how good they were against Iowa in the Sun Carnival Basketball Tournament in December of 1965. We had played some good teams but hadn't played anyone ranked. Iowa was ranked No. 3.

65

After ten minutes of play, we had Iowa 32–4. They'd made only four three throws. Their first field goal came by accident, with Shed tipping the ball. We totally dominated the game and won 86–68. It was really worse than the score indicated.

I was surprised that we could handle such a great team so easily and I still consider that game the start to our championship.

Not that I was thinking national title yet. That came a couple of weeks later. We went to Arizona State and beat a real good Sun Devils team. One of my friends over there, Dow Wigginton who had played at Oklahoma State, told me that "if your guys keep improving they'll have a chance to win the whole thing." It began to dawn on me then that we might have that type of ball club.

Not that they were an easy bunch to coach. They wouldn't play hard all the time. As we won more and more games they got cockier and cockier.

Because of that we had some close games that never should have been close. They plain drove me crazy.

Seventeen

ONE OF THE GREATEST GAMES I've ever seen was our game against University of New Mexico during that 1966 season.

We were down by nineteen points. We came back to win 67–64 in overtime. At that time the sport was much slower. Getting ahead by nineteen points these days may not be much because of the shot clock and the quickness of the game. But it was a big thing then.

New Mexico had as good a team as there was in the nation. If there was a team which I would have hated to play in the NCAA playoffs it was New Mexico.

Utah edged the Lobos out for the Western Athletic Conference title and went into the play-offs. Utah made it to the Final Four. Utah was good, too, but not as good as New Mexico.

We went undefeated until the final game of the regular season. We lost 74–72 to University of Seattle at Seattle. We had a better team but it was one of those games in which our guys didn't play hard. Not that Seattle wasn't good. It could have been a Final Four team. Hill didn't play very well. He and Cager spent all night trying to take the ball to the basket and the officials weren't calling any fouls. When officials aren't calling anything you have to get out of your game plan and try something else.

I was a bit worried at the time because we were to play a very good Oklahoma City team in the first round of the NCAA play-offs the next week. But as it turned out, the loss to Seattle was a good thing. It showed our players that they could get beat. We wound up the regular season with a 23–1 record.

Oklahoma City had the leading rebounder in the nation, a fellow by the name of "Big Game" Hunter, and a great guard. It was probably the best team Abe Lemons ever had as a coach.

We played the first part of that game without Hill. He

had missed curfew and I didn't start him. We were getting beat pretty good and I had to finally put him in the game. He scored seventeen points in about seven minutes and we won 89–74.

Our next game was in the Regional Tournament against Cincinnati, which hadn't got much credit but was one of the best teams we played all year. They were so well balanced I can't remember a single player's name. They had us down with about seven minutes to go, just like a lot of teams did that season.

We came back and won 78–76 in overtime and were very lucky to do so.

The best team we played all year was Kansas, our opponent in the next game. They had Jo Jo White and Walt Wesley. I still think that game was for the national championship. If Kansas had beat us, Kansas would have gone all the way.

The final score was 81–80. White made a basket from the sideline right after the final buzzer. A lot of people watching the game on television thought the shot counted. But he had one foot out-of-bounds and, besides, the whistle had blown. Those of us on the sideline knew the shot was no good. It was really no big deal. Even if he'd been in-bounds it wouldn't have counted.

We had a hard time defensing Kansas because they were so much bigger. But Hill did a pretty good job on White. Wesley, on the other hand, was a seven-footer and we had no one near that size.

Jerry Armstrong was a key man for us in our first game in the Final Four at College Park, Maryland, against Utah. We didn't play very well and Jerry Chambers was eating us up. Armstrong went into the game and despite a sprained ankle actually won the game for us. My other big guys had all gotten into foul trouble. Armstrong did a better job of guarding Chambers than the other guys.

Chambers was a great shooter and wound up with over thirty points. But without Armstrong he would have scored more and we never would have gotten into the championship game.

Beating Kentucky wasn't really all that much of a thrill. We'd had a long season and played a lot of great teams.

Like I said before, my players drove me crazy with their confidence. They thought they could beat anybody. I kept trying to convince them they would have to play hard against Kentucky but they didn't believe me.

I guess it was a good thing. They didn't put any pressure on themselves and were loose.

We hadn't scouted Kentucky. Our recruiting budget was still only $5,000 and we didn't have enough money to scout anybody. We went up against Kentucky cold turkey.

Kentucky came out with a 1–3–1 trapping zone defense. That was the first time we had played against it. I called time out and tried to tell our players what to do. My main strategy was to attack the 1–3–1. I also told them to practice as the game went along.

Most teams would have been scared to death but not these guys. They were handling the 1–3–1 easily before long. Hill was a big help, telling our players what to do as the situation warranted.

We beat Kentucky 72–65 but there wasn't the emotion you'd expect after winning a national championship. The players just knew they were going to win so it wasn't that big a deal. Not at the time. I think as they look back on it they think differently.

As for me, I was just happy it was over. It had been a long season and I was emotionally drained.

I rate Hill as one of the best guards ever to play basketball. He and Nate Archibald were very much alike. Both were lefthanded, both could penetrate, both were good shooters and both played great defense.

Hill could have gone on to the NBA but he had no desire to do so. He dropped out of school the next year and got married.

Eighteen

THE YEAR AFTER WE WON the national championship I went to New York to see the 125-pound player named Nate Archibald.

You'd think I would still be flying high over winning the national championship, but I wasn't. I was really depressed over all the hate mail and adverse publicity we had received.

I had a good friend by the name of Bill Cornwall. He traveled with us everywhere and he would sit on the bench with us. He owned Cornwall Supply Co. in El Paso.

He had a great sense of humor and could really pick me up when I was down. He made the trip with me to New York to see Archibald.

I didn't feel much like talking but I was still being interviewed a lot due to our national championship. Bill would answer the phone for me and pretend he was me.

"Yeah, yeah," he would say, "this is Don Haskins. What can I do for you?"

Then they'd start asking him questions and he'd answer them as well as I could. He knew me so well he knew what I would say. He even talked on national radio pretending he was me.

That would really crack me up and it helped me pick up my spirits.

Incidentally, Cornwall was having eye problems at the time and eventually went completely blind.

Archibald was playing in the finals of the high school basketball play-offs. There was another player on his team who everybody considered the big prize. His last name was Robinson. He was six feet four and some player.

There was little old Archibald out on the floor with him, all arms and legs. He was about five-ten then and they called him "Tiny."

I fell in love with him then and there.

There was another player on the team I brought back with Archibald. His name was Mike Switzer. He had a lot of potential, but he didn't work anywhere near as hard as Archibald.

When we had practice at, say, 3:30 P.M., Switzer would show up at 3:25.

Archibald would show up at 11:00 A.M.

Of course, Nate's progress was unbelievable. He just kept getting better and better.

I wish I could give myself credit for his development, but I can't. He was a self-made player.

Not only did he show up early for practice, he'd stay after practice. Many times he wouldn't even eat lunch. He'd come in at 11:00 A.M., we'd practice at 3:30 and when I would

71

leave my office at eight o'clock at night I'd see him out in the gym still practicing. He did that every day.

When he got to Texas Western I had a frank talk with him. I said, "Nate, there's one thing that you can't do. You can't shoot."

He could take the ball to the basket. He had learned that on the playgrounds in New York. But he couldn't even make free throws.

He made up his mind he was going to learn. And he did, by working hours and hours and hours.

He took excellent care of himself. He was like Lattin in that respect. He didn't drink or smoke. I couldn't even get him to have a glass of wine when he would come to my house for dinner.

There's no doubt that he's one of the greatest guards who ever lived. Jim Williams, coach at Colorado State, made the comment once that Nate Archibald was the only guard he ever saw who could dominate a game. He said he's seen big men dominate, but not a guard.

Archibald broke Barnes' school record for most points scored in a career and holds the school record for most field goals made. And what a free throw shooter he became. He not only set a school record for most free throws made with 559, but ranks second in all-time free throw percentage with .780.

He played many years in the NBA and is one of only twelve lefthanders ever to score more than twelve thousand points. That's a big accomplishment for a guard in pro basketball.

Only two athletes have had their numbers at Texas Western retired. One was Barnes' No. 45.

The other was Archibald's No. 14.

By the way, Texas Western's name was changed to University of Texas at El Paso the year after we won the national championship. It had nothing to do with our title. The Texas system decided to change the names of all of its branch schools at that time. Thus we now have University of Texas at El Paso, University of Texas at Arlington, and so on.

Our school is now often referred to simply as UTEP.

Nineteen

THE NEXT YEAR, THE 1966–67 SEASON, we went 22–8. No telling what we would have done if we had had Bobby Joe Hill all season.

He was with us part of the season but he was hurt and he was married and he was confused. He wouldn't go to school half the time. He suffered a groin pull and charley horses in both legs. He was off the team at mid-term.

But I still think he was as good as Archibald and could have played in the NBA. Bobby Joe is as tough a leader as I've ever had.

Archibald and Hill were different as day and night in personality, though. Like I say, Archibald didn't drink. Bobby Joe did, and he used to kid about it.

I remember one incident very well. I walked in the dorm one day looking for somebody. The door to Bobby Joe's room was partly open. I saw him sitting there with his feet on the table and a big bottle of Mogen David wine on it. He was just a sophomore.

Don Davis and a couple of other football players were sitting there with him. Bobby Joe was talking big as usual and using a few profanities. He was drinking wine out of a big cup.

He had his back to me. Davis and the other players saw me and fell silent. Bobby Joe turned around and his jaw dropped.

Boy, was I mad. I grabbed him by the shirt and pulled him up. I gave him a royal chewing out.

The next day I took him to the gym and ran him until he got sick. He fell on the floor and threw up all over Memorial Gym. Nevil Shed came over and tried to help him get up. I told Shed to get the hell out of there.

A couple of players we were trying to recruit came by just about then and saw what was going on. I never saw them again.

It was terrible. I don't know if I'd do that now.

I told Bobby Joe that if he quit running before I told him to stop, he was off the team. He fell before he would quit. That's how tough he was.

He was a fancy dan on the court and I tried to break him of it. He wasn't a showoff, but he would dribble behind his back and between his legs. I would get after him and he'd just get more and more confused. He didn't know any other way to play. That's how he learned on the playgrounds; that's how he grew up playing.

Finally, I got smart and told him to play his game. There was no stopping him after that.

He had as quick a first step as I've ever seen. He could penetrate any defense, just like Archibald.

He's been working for El Paso Natural Gas Company for over twenty years. He must be awfully happy there to have stayed so long.

74

Don Haskins and his wife, Mary, with their four sons. From left: Brent, Don, Steve, David, Mary and Mark. This photo was taken in El Paso in 1966 shortly after Haskins led Texas Western to the NCAA Championship.

The Iba family figured prominently in Coach Haskins' career. At left is Moe Iba. Moe's father, Henry Iba, is in center.

Key players in the early years of Haskins' tenure with the Miners were (from left) Willie Brown, Bobby Lesley and Nolan Richardson

Jim "Bad News" Barnes still holds several scoring record at UTEP. He led the Miners to a 25–3 record in the 1963–6 season.

Haskins has been known to have a few words with officials during his twenty-six years on the job, as this picture demonstrates.

The 1966 NCAA championship team, left to right: front row —
Bobby Joe Hill, Orsten Artis, Togo Railey, Willie Worsley; second
row — David Palacio, Dick Myers, Harry Flournoy, Louis
Baudoin; third row — Nevil Shed, Jerry Armstrong, Willie Cager,
David Lattin, Coach Don Haskins. Below: The team posed in the
same order at a 1986 reunion in El Paso. Eddie Mullens, standing
at right foreground, directed the session.

Twenty

ALTHOUGH WE WENT 22–8 in 1966–67, you'd think it was a horrible record the way some people talked. I guess that was normal after winning a national championship.

Besides losing Bobby Joe Hill at midterm, we lost Harry Flournoy and Orsten Artis through graduation.

Still, we got some good wins. We won our first five games before losing 71–62 to a strong University of New Mexico team. Then we beat Kansas and Wichita State before losing to Southern Illinois. The Salukis were in the middle of a strong program then. We beat both Arizona and Arizona State.

And in the last game of the season we got revenge on Seattle, which had handed us our only loss the year before. This time we beat Seattle 62–54.

We went up against University of Pacific in our first NCAA playoff game and they beat us 72–63. Nevil Shed was in his fourth year. Shed had played in the NCAA playoffs with North Carolina A&T and at that time there was a rule that you couldn't play four years. A player could play only his sophomore, junior and senior years.

Shed played with us during the season since we were independent but wasn't eligible for the play-offs.

So we had Freddie Carr take his place. He had been

recruited for basketball but had turned into a whale of a football player.

He did a good job. In fact, he wound up as the second leading rebounder in the regional tournament behind Lew Alcindor, now known as Kareem Abdul-Jabbar.

We played University of Wyoming in the consolation game. Wyoming had won the Western Athletic Conference championship and we beat them, 68–67.

Carr had seven tip-ins in that game.

Alcindor and UCLA were unbeatable. Nobody came close to them that year. They beat Pacific pretty easily and went on to the national title.

Archibald was already in our fold but he couldn't play that season because of the three-year rule. I sent him to Marion Moss, who was coaching Arizona Western Junior College. I also sent Switzer to him. I knew Moss was a good friend and would help me protect them. Moss had played with me in college.

With Archibald and Switzer on the team, Arizona Western beat the hell out of people. They were something like 28–2.

Arizona and Arizona State got wind of Archibald and Switzer and went after them. Moss was great. He wouldn't even let them see their transcripts.

Twenty One

WE WENT 14–9 in Archibald's first year on the team. That was the 1967–68 season.

Nate was just a sophomore and still very small. In fact, our whole team was small.

Archibald was a heck of a dribbler and could do many other things well. But like I said before he couldn't shoot well. We talked a lot about his shooting. I told him he had no excuse not to be a good shooter because now he could have a ball to practice with.

The way he grew up, in the playgrounds of New York, kids didn't have enough balls to practice their shooting. In fact, there'd be maybe one old ball for fifty kids. The only way they got to see action was to wait their turns. It would be five against five. The five who won would stay on the court and the losers would sit down. If your fivesome didn't win, you didn't see much action.

Archibald must have taken my advice to heart. He began practicing and soon was spending more time shooting the ball than any player I've ever been associated with. He'd shoot for something like seven or eight hours a day.

He kept it up through his three years at UTEP and by the time he got to the National Basketball Association he hit his peak.

He would practice on those little baskets that I mentioned earlier. I had Paul Barry of Wyler Industrial in El Paso fix some up for me. He'd cut down the regular rims so that the ball would barely fit. On a regular rim, you can squeeze two balls through.

I noticed something. The guys who really practiced their shooting and became good shots would work on those little rims. The guys who couldn't shoot wouldn't.

Archibald got where he could make seven or eight free throws out of ten on the little rim, and that is a fantastic percentage.

He also worked hard on other parts of his game. Here he was, already a great dribbler. He would come out on the floor each day dribbling. He would dribble down the sideline righthanded then would go across the court lefthanded and back down the sideline. He'd stop and go. Just fundamentals, no fancy stuff like behind the back and all that.

He'd do that for about twenty minutes. Then he'd shoot from one side, then the other. He'd bank some in, he'd shoot free throws.

All this, of course, was before regular practice.

He reminded me of what Lee Trevino once told me. I saw Lee on a practice tee one day with a huge stack of balls at his side. He was hitting and hitting and sweating like crazy.

He saw me looking at him, and he said, "Coach, you know it's real funny, but the more of these I hit the luckier I get."

Another athlete who reminds me of Archibald is the Boston Celtics' Larry Bird. He'll go out and shoot for two hours before a game. I don't recommend that for my players. I like for them to be sharp. But Bird is a workaholic, and Archibald was the same way. That's why they will go down as great players.

Although the 14–9 record was the worst I'd had as a college coach up to that time I wasn't disappointed. Not only were we awfully small but we were hurting in recruiting because of that negative publicity we'd had. We couldn't get any big players. The only reason we got Archibald was because he was small and wasn't highly recruited.

Another thing that hurt us was the fact we were splitting up our games between our home gym (Memorial) and the El Paso County Coliseum.

Our biggest player was Dick Gibbs, who was six feet five and a half. Other players included Switzer at six-four, Andrew White at six-three and Ples Vann, six-four. Archibald was only five-eleven then.

We scored a lot of points. We scored over eighty points in seven games and over ninety in one. But we couldn't stop anybody on the offensive boards because of our size.

Twenty Two

WE HAD THE SAME PROBLEM during the 1968–69 season. We won sixteen games and lost nine.

We gave Archibald, now a junior, the ball and let him go. He was getting better and better.

Like I said, we were small, but boy, were we fast. But lack of size hurt us on defense.

I guess the fans and boosters liked our style of play. Some people might think there would have been complaints for our not having better records after winning the national championship but there were few that I know of.

We were still splitting our games between Memorial Gym and the Coliseum. The facilities at the Coliseum were horrible. There were no dressing rooms and there were loose boards on the floor of the court. We never practiced there so it was like playing away from home.

Crazy thing, though, we did real well there, winning a lot of our games.

The reason we played there, of course, is because it had a bigger seating capacity. You could fit in over eight thousand spectators.

Although I didn't like the Coliseum facilities, I loved the fans who went there when we played. I've always had a place in my heart for the middle class. The Coliseum is situated in a poorer part of town than where UTEP is located.

We'd go down there early and there were a bunch of fans, mostly Mexican-Americans, already on hand. They'd be out in the parking lot waiting for us, having little picnics.

I really miss that. It was a real mixture of El Paso, everything from country clubbers to poor folks.

Some seats went for only $2.

We have a 12,222-seat Special Events Center now. I wish we could set aside about 1,000 seats for $2 so we could get many of those poorer people into our games now.

There are no better fans than Hispanics. They really holler for you and get behind you. There were some hot times at the Coliseum. I remember one time we were playing University of Arizona. This Hispanic fellow came onto the floor and went after one of the Arizona players who had done something or other. We and the Wildcats were bitter rivals then, anyway. The fans really got on them. The police took this fellow off and I don't know what became of him.

I enjoyed those picnics in the parking lot very much. Many a time I sat down with some of the fans and had a burrito or a taco. They'd offer me some beer, too, but I couldn't have any before a game. Not that I didn't want one.

I hate to make public speeches, but I really enjoyed just sitting down and talking to those fans.

Twenty Three

UTEP HAD BEEN TRYING for some time to get into the Western Athletic Conference. Finally, it succeeded in 1969. That meant our first season in the WAC would be the 1969–70 season — Archibald's senior year.

It suited us just fine. We won the conference championship in our first season, thanks to Archibald.

I'll never forget our first two conference games. They were on the road. Our first opponent was Colorado State. They played us man to man and Archibald ate them up. He scored over thirty points. We won 77–64.

The next night we were at Wyoming. They didn't know about Archibald yet, either, and they played us man to man, too. Archibald went to town again and scored over thirty points once more. We won 80–70.

We never saw a man to man defense in WAC play that season again. Everybody used a zone defense.

The conference championship was on the line in the last game of the season against University of Utah. The winner would walk away with the title. The game was held before 8,500 screaming fans at El Paso Coliseum.

We were down seven points with a minute-and-a-half to go. Then Archibald took over and played what I still consider the greatest minute-and-a-half I've ever seen anyone play.

We started pressing at that point. We stole the ball and Archibald scored. We stole the ball again and Archibald scored. Utah's best free throw shooter missed a free throw and Archibald scored.

We stole the ball again and he scored.

At the end of the game, we had the ball again.

Archibald had scored all eight points in that minute-and-a-half and we won 83–82.

We went into the NCAA tournament after that without Dick Gibbs, our six feet five and a half center. He was hurt. We went from a small team to a midget team.

We scored a lot of points against Utah State, but they scored more. Final score was 91–81.

Gibbs was a good player and went in the second round of the draft.

As for Archibald, he was selected to play in post-season tournaments. Those all-star games were right up Archibald's alley because teams have to play man to man.

His first appearance was in the East-West game. He scored thirty-five points.

Then came the Aloha Classic. I took him aside before he went to that one. He was so unselfish he never put up more than fifteen shots during a game. I told him, "Tiny, I know

86

this isn't the way you play basketball but you be a little more selfish. To get into the NBA you're going to have to show them that you can score some points."

He went over and scored over forty points in one game and fifty-three in another.

He was named Most Valuable Player in the tournament.

I had called Bob Cousy, the former Boston Celtics great, and told him about Archibald. I figured he would appreciate Archibald despite his size because Cousy was small, too.

Cousy was coach for the Cincinnati Royals. He went to the Aloha Classic and saw him play. The Royals drafted him in the second round and he went on to become a superstar in the National Basketball Association.

Incidentally, one year Archibald told me he was going to lead the NBA in both scoring and assists. It had never been done before.

He went out and did it. I still consider it one of the most unbelievable feats ever in the NBA.

He never tried to do it again. He just played.

Everytime I think of Archibald predicting he would lead the NBA in scoring and assists I think of Babe Ruth and the time he pointed where he was going to hit a homerun.

Twenty Four

I'VE BEEN LUCKY to have some great people helping me through the years. One of the most outstanding people in that respect is the late Ross Moore.

He had been the trainer at Texas Western before I got there and remained in that position until his death in 1977. He was more than a trainer, though. He was the most competitive person I've been around — ever. He made trips with us and would get on the officials mercilessly.

But he was very protective of our players. I had gotten to be like Henry Iba. I would tell the players we would go shoot "for a little while" the day of the game then I'd keep them out there for hours if I saw something I didn't like. I was doing as a coach the very things I hated when I was a player.

Moore used to call me "Sonny." Whenever I called for a practice the day of a game he would come over to me and say, "Sonny, I'm going to go over to the gym with the fellers and have a little shooting practice. Why don't you just hang around here."

In other words, he was telling me to stay the hell away from the practice so the players could just shoot some.

The players all loved him, of course.

He was just like a mother hen in other ways. He used to watch over each player when he ate. He saw that they got the right amounts of food, that they didn't get too much of this or too little of that.

In the old days, steaks were the thing. It was believed they were the right food for athletes. Well, David Lattin didn't like steaks. He would rather eat scrambled eggs. They had a lot of hassles over that and I think they sort of compromised.

Come game time, this old mother hen Moore turned into a terror. I can't begin to count how many technical fouls he got which, of course, were credited to me by the news media.

He got me kicked out of one game in Wyoming. He kept after me to get on this one particular official, all the while getting on all of them himself.

Me, I was mad at the players and getting on them. I wasn't getting on the officials because I didn't think my players were playing hard enough to warrant it. The officiating wasn't that good but the players weren't working at it too hard, either.

Moore kept telling me, "Aren't you going to do something about the officiating?" and "When in the hell are you going to do something?"

Finally, I did do something. I had gotten sick and tired of hearing him yell at me. I went out and got me three technicals, which automatically got me thrown out of the game.

I walked by Moore as I left the court, waved to him and told him, "Okay, now you do this any damn way you want to."

Darn if he didn't end up winning the game by a point.

Another time we were playing at Memorial Gym. I remember the official at the time very well. It was Irv Brown, who later became a nationally-ranked official and television announcer.

I didn't know Irv very well then. He was very tough on home crowds and was never intimidated.

It was a game again in which I wasn't too unhappy with the officiating but Moore was. He kept after the officials, and especially Irv. I kept telling Moore to take it easy but he wouldn't listen.

I warned Moore that he was going to get us a technical if he didn't settle down and that we weren't playing that well anyway.

"No, the officiating isn't any good," he said. And he kept it up.

Pretty soon Irv Brown came by the bench. When Brown gets aggravated his forehead gets really wrinkled. Boy, was it wrinkled now. He pointed to us and declared a technical on the bench.

I got upset about that and went to half-court to talk to Brown. I said, "Irv . . ."

He turned around and said, "What in the hell are you doing here. I just called a technical on your trainer."

I said, "I know that, but I want everybody in Memorial Gym to know that. I keep getting blamed for these technical fouls."

Brown said, "Get back to the bench. You're embarrassing me."

I told him, "You're going to have to throw me out of the game. All I want you to do is come down in front of my bench, blow your whistle, quiet everybody down and announce so everyone can hear that the technical foul is on Ross Moore."

He said okay and walked down to the bench. I stood by him in front of Moore and he did just as I asked him.

Moore slumped down on his seat, meek as a kitten. "That's a dirty trick," he told me, "I can't believe you did that."

That slowed him down for a game or two but he was back getting me technicals again before long.

90

Overall, he got more technical fouls in the years he was with me than I did.

Moore had graduate assistants and both turned out to be great trainers, too.

Succeeding Moore was Don Forrester. Don was not only a fine trainer but had a tremendous singing voice. He sang the National Anthem at many of our games.

But he, too, got me some technicals.

Forrester left us to go into business and then came Dave Binder.

If you lined up all the trainers in the country today and asked me to choose one, I would pick Binder. He has been just terrific.

Trainers can be a big help to a coach in many ways. They get to know more about players than coaches do. They learn the players' idiosyncrasies and personal lives a lot better than a coach. Naturally, players behave around their coach. But they let their hair down around a trainer.

I used to have a very outstanding player named Gary Brewster. He was hard to talk to. I would call him in my office and try to talk to him but he would just turn his head.

He didn't pal around with any of the players. Binder, however, got to be his friend while he was an assistant trainer. They'd go out together. It helped Brewster feel more comfortable, I'm sure.

Incidentally, years later Brewster would come by my office to visit and I couldn't get him out. He really changed.

There are a lot of other examples. When I want to know something personal about a player I go to the trainer. They know the gripers, the ones who are having problems, the ones who seem to have personality conflicts.

Players can fool a coach but not a trainer. Sometimes I

91

have thought a player is a smart aleck but then I find out from the trainer he's not.

David Lattin looked like a big, surly type. But Moore got along with him and was the first to tell me he was a good kid. He was right, of course.

Trainers are something like father confessors, too. Players go to them with their problems and trainers do everything they can to help them.

I can't say enough about how important trainers are to a team.

Twenty Five

ASSISTANT COACHES are invaluable, too, of course.

The very first one I had at Texas Western was Tom Rush. He was the one and only assistant coach I had my first year and he did it for the love of the game. The college didn't pay him a dime.

He not only helped me with the varsity but he coached the freshman team. Freshman teams were allowed in those days.

Tom worked for the City Recreation Department and later became a high school coach. And a darn good one.

El Paso has had some really outstanding high school coaches in addition to Rush. One of them is C. D. Jarvis, who coached at El Paso High School. He won a state championship and I don't know how many district titles. What a great baskeball mind he had.

He could have coached in college if he had wanted to. I'll tell you how dedicated he was. He retired after forty years of coaching. During his fortieth year, he attended a coaches' clinic. There he was about to retire and he was still trying to pick up scraps of information on coaching.

Then there were Tom Chavez at El Paso Jefferson High, Bobby Lesley at El Paso Eastwood, Alvis Glidewell at El Paso Austin, Nemo Herrera at El Paso Bowie, Ed Haller who also coached at Austin, Buddy Moore at Ysleta, John Leonard and Joe Anderson at El Paso Irvin.

All those guys could have coached at the college level if they'd wanted to. Some coaches like to stay in the high school ranks, however.

But getting back to my assistant coaches.

Rush was with me that first year then I got a paid assistant. It was Moe Iba, a son of Henry Iba. I got Moe right out of college. He was only twenty-two but he had his dad's basketball mind. I still say he's the best scout I've ever seen. He could scout a team once and tell you everything about it, and what options you had.

He didn't have much experience, of course, but he learned quickly. He was a darn good recruiter, too. He was responsible for recruiting most of the players on our 1966 national championship team.

Our winning the national title helped him get a head coaching job. It's funny, but when a team wins a national championship an assistant coach can almost pick his spot as to where to coach.

He went to Memphis State and did a great job. Then he moved to University of Nebraska.

93

I'm sure it's tough coaching basketball at Nebraska. That's a football school and it's won some national titles. A basketball coach there is constantly being compared to the football coach.

I had known Moe since I was in college and had liked him even then. Of course, since I went to Oklahoma A&M and since George McCarty knew Henry Iba, getting Moe to come to Texas Western was only natural.

We got along great and I still consider myself fortunate to have had him.

By the way, he got quite a few technical fouls, too. It seems to be my lot in life to absorb technicals of trainers and assistant coaches.

My next assistant after Moe was Jerry Hale. He had taken my place at Dumas High School when I left to take the job at Texas Western. I helped him get that job. He was just getting out of Oklahoma A&M and I had met him there. Knowing he had played under Henry Iba made my recommending him to Dumas that much easier.

Jerry, by the way, took my team at Dumas, the players I had put together, and won the state championship.

When I called Jerry to offer him the job as my assistant I was surprised he had become somewhat disenchanted and was thinking of dropping out of coaching. But he finally came and did a super job while with me.

The College of Idaho, one of the best junior colleges in the nation, then beckoned. Eddie Sutton, later head coach at University of Arkansas and University of Kentucky, had been coaching there and had left. Hale took his place.

Jerry eventually wound up at Oral Roberts.

Ed Sparling succeeded Jerry as my assistant. Sparling was regarded as one of the finest junior college coaches around in those days.

Sparling was a great offensive coach. While with me he kind of got turned around and went totally defense. I've laughed about that.

I got Dick Gibbs along with Sparling. He had been playing for Sparling at Burlington Junior College in Iowa.

And I almost got another great player. Freddy "Downtown" Brown had been playing for Sparling, too. He went on to play many years in the NBA with the Seattle Super Sonics.

If we had gotten Brown we would have had him and Archibald on the same team as guards. What a combination that would have been.

We didn't get Brown but we did get another player with Sparling. He was Charley Brakes, a fine player who helped us a lot.

My next assistant coach was Gene Iba, a nephew of Henry Iba's. I was kind of hesitant to take another Iba but Mr. Iba talked to me. The thing that sold me on Gene is that with an all-white team he won the city high school championship in St. Louis. That just isn't done.

Gene turned out to be one of the finest college coaches in the country. Not only did he do a great job for us but he went on to do a super job as head coach at Houston Baptist. He had winning teams there, and took the school into the NCAA tournament a couple of times.

He later became head coach at Baylor University.

Gene and I made a bad combination when it came to recruiting, though. I've always been perfectly honest with high school players and Gene was the same way. We both believed in telling kids the bad side of coming to our school. We told it exactly as it was. Other coaches at least tell them they can have some fun. All we told them was the misery, that they had to attend class, that they had to do this and that. I don't think that between the two of us we ever told anyone what they *could* do.

But the kids we got that way were workers and we had some good teams.

Gene was an honest, hard working type that any president of a university would be proud to have at the school.

Twenty Six

WHICH BRINGS ME TO TIM FLOYD, my assistant from 1976 to 1986.

He is probably the best recruiter I've ever known. And he knew how to get the town involved with our team. What a worker. If he had just one dollar for every hour he spent working after 5:00 P.M. he'd be a rich man.

For years I never let my players go anywhere. Nate Archibald never went to anyone's house for dinner. I just wouldn't allow anyone to get close to our players.

Tim changed all that. He got our players to knowing people. I think that has helped people get to know our team better and at the same time make the players feel more at ease, more like they're at home.

I almost didn't hire Tim. He has the worst handwriting in the world. He was attending Louisiana Tech and wrote me a letter asking for a job as a graduate assistant.

I read the first paragraph and the writing was so awful I was about to throw it in the waste paper basket. But the name "Lee Floyd" caught my eye. In the second paragraph Tim wrote, "You might remember my dad, Lee Floyd."

If Tim had put that sentence at the end of his letter I never would have seen it because I wouldn't have got down that far.

Well, I did remember his dad. Lee Floyd had been a great athlete and coached at Mississippi Southern for years. He got arthritis real bad and retired in El Paso. He would come to our practices and games often.

Because of Lee, I finished reading Tim's letter as best I could. I wound up hiring him because judging by his handwriting it looked like the kid really needed help.

Tim began at a very low wage. We had his annual salary up to $10,000 before long, which still wasn't much but was an improvement.

Abe Lemons, then head coach at University of Texas, learned about the good job Tim was doing for us and offered him $30,000 to become his assistant.

Ed Swartz had become athletic director at UTEP. Ed was much maligned. A lot of people didn't understand him and he didn't last very long, but he certainly helped me. I'll always appreciate him.

It wasn't often that I got a raise, except for a cost of living adjustment. I hadn't met Swartz yet but one day soon after he took over he called me and said, "I just looked at your salary, and I want to give you a $6,000 a year raise."

I've heard at times that "you can't do this or you can't do that." Swartz never said that. I asked him if he could raise Tim's salary to a respectable level. He called me back and said he could get Tim $26,000.

That was a $16,000 raise and Tim decided to stay.

Tim was worth every penny, and more. He used to wear me out recruiting. He never took "no" for an answer. He would have me go out to talk with some players and we wouldn't get back until 11:00 P.M. I'd be dog-tired when I got to bed.

"Persistent" is too soft a word to describe him.

At this writing, Tim is head coach at University of Idaho. I know one thing. He'll be getting Idaho some good players.

And he'll do awfully well with them. He learned about coaching the years he was at UTEP. When I was starting out as coach I used to do all the coaching myself. I changed my philosophy and let Tim do some of it himself. He filled in for me during illnesses and did an outstanding job.

But really, success all starts with recruiting. I remember the time I was sitting at Coronado Country Club with some friends. Darrell Royal, the highly successful head football coach at University of Texas, had two 6–4 seasons and people were beginning to get on him.

A couple of the friends I was sitting with were Texas exes. One of them said Darrell Royal was getting "too old." Another said, "Yeah, and he messes around with that country western music too much. He has too many business interests."

The next year, I was sitting with the same guys the day after Royal had won the Cotton Bowl and the Longhorns had been declared national champions. I asked them what they thought of Royal now.

They looked at me like I was crazy. Why, they didn't remember saying he was "too old" or had "too many business interests" and they thought he was the greatest coach in the world.

So you see, with such a talent for recruiting Tim figures to do well. And I guess he'll stay "young" for many years.

Nate Archibald's number was retired by the Miners. He's shown here with his wife, Jean, during ceremonies at the Special Events Center.

Assistant coach Tim Floyd was a hard working recruiter for the Miners and put out a lot of effort during games as well.

Coach Haskins is surrounded by Paul Cunningham, Fred Reynolds and Anthony Bailey (left to right) after another Sun Bowl victory.

Juden Smith, Donnell Allen and Kevin Hamilton (left to right) helped the Miners reach new heights during the 1980s.

The late Ross Moore was more than just a trainer with the Miners. He helped players with personal problems and looked after their needs.

Luster Goodwin helped the Miners win WAC titles with his deadly outside shooting. Here he displays his shooting form.

Jim Forbes not only played for the Miners but played for the United States Olympic team. A knee injury snuffed out a promising professional career.

Beto Bautista, an El Paso product, was a teammate of Forbes'. Haskins rates him as one of the top hustlers he's ever coached.

Coach Don Haskins, right, has had some tense moments. At extreme left is announcer Paul Strelzin. Next to Haskins is trainer Dave Binder.

Twenty Seven

TO BE SUCCESSFUL, a coach must have the backing of the community in which he works. I've been lucky in that respect.

Lindsay Holt, who is one of the best businessmen I've ever known, has been extremely helpful for years.

Holt founded the El Dorados, the school's booster club. He got people from throughout El Paso together to help the Miners. They've raised thousands upon thousands of dollars for the athletic program.

Holt began as an employee at Architectural Products Co. and worked his way up. Now, he's owner of the company.

But Holt has been more than a business acquaintance.

He has become a personal friend. And he has helped in many different ways.

Terry White, who played for us in the late 1970s, was having problems with a roommate and was thinking of leaving El Paso. Holt took him into his home, became his legal guardian and treated him just like his own son. Holt has done everything possible within NCAA rules to help me and my players.

Another great friend is Stretch Elliott, who was quite an athlete in his own right. He lettered in both baseball and basketball at University of Virginia but his real strength was in football. He was an end at Virginia then played four years at that position for the Green Bay Packers.

He's a successful businessman, too. He moved to El Paso in the 1940s and went into the insurance business. He has his own agency now.

He has been to almost as many of our team's practices as I have. He comes by my office four or five times a week and has been doing that almost since the day I arrived on the campus.

He really gets excited at our games. His face is all splotched up after a game. He looks worse than I do, and I look pretty bad after a game.

I first met Elliott at a civic function. After our next game, he came to the dressing room and invited me out for a drink.

We visit back and forth even now. A man couldn't ask for a better friend.

Dr. Bill Dickey, our team physician, and Bill Cornwall are others who have been close friends and a great help to me.

I don't like to talk to people about my troubles. These fellows have done a lot of sticking up for me.

Cornwall is one of the finest fellows I've ever met. He used to make me mad because he wouldn't sit on our bench during a home game. Like I said, he was losing his sight and eventually became blind. He didn't like to be led into the gym. Still, he would come to the games and Dr. Dickey would tell him what was going on.

Cornwall didn't let his failing eyesight stand in the way of his humor. He was always making me laugh. He could mimic other people to perfection. He could have been a comedian on the stage.

I also want to mention a couple of women in the administrative office who were really supercompetent.

They're Cathy Bates and Marge Williamson.

Cathy was McCarty's secretary and later worked in the Dean of Men's Office. Marge is the school's ticket manager.

Wayne Vandenburg, our track coach, and I used to drive them absolutely crazy.

Vandenburg is one of the most talented persons I've ever met. He was a great promoter and a heck of a good guy in addition to being a good coach. He could do anything.

But we were both terrible at turning in expense account vouchers. I would go six months without turning in one. They used to get after me and I'd put it off and put it off.

The other day I took out an old sports jacket and I felt something in it. I took it out and it was a receipt from 1969 that I had forgotten to turn in.

Cathy and Marge somehow or another got me through it all. Cathy probably called hotels to check and get receipts.

Wayne was a bit worse than I, but not much.

Not that we did it intentionally. We did a lot of traveling. I would come back from a trip fully intending to list my expenses and turn in the receipts but then I had to go on another trip the following week. Before I knew it, I had five trips to list and by that time I'd misplaced the receipts or forgotten what I'd done.

If you do it right, you turn in the stuff right after a trip but Wayne and I wouldn't do that.

We're lucky we didn't get fired. Cathy and Marge probably saved our jobs.

Dr. Arleigh Templeton, president of the university in the late 1970s, deserves a lot of praise, too. If it hadn't been for him we may never had got the Special Events Center built.

He was very controversial. The first time I met him he told, me, "I'm going to be the most controversial person you've ever met."

105

He was, but he was also a doer. You have to make things happen in the state capital in Austin to get things done and he did. He hadn't been here long before we got the Special Events Center. And he had a lot of other things built.

The Special Events Center has really helped in our recruiting. In fact, it saved basketball at UTEP. Big basketball arenas were springing up around the Southwest then. Suddenly there was the Pan American Center at New Mexico State and The Pit at University of New Mexico. University of Arizona and Arizona State got new places, too.

And there we were in little old Memorial Gym.

There's a lot of difference trying to get a player to come to Memorial Gym or to the Special Events Center. Memorial Gym looked okay when it was packed. But when there wasn't a game the seats would be pulled back and it looked awful. It didn't even look like a place to play basketball. We could see the disappointment in the players' faces when we took them there.

The Special Events Center looks good with or without a crowd. Of course, it looks even better with people in there and we try to bring in recruits during a game. They see over 12,000 people yelling and screaming. It's exciting and we've landed quite a few players because of it.

We've had other fine team doctors in addition to Dr. Dickey. Some who have traveled with us include Dr. Bob Snyder, Dr. Tim Lambert, Dr. Hampton Briggs and Dr. Jim Hampton. They've all meant an awful lot to our program.

I've had some good times with Martin Lettunich, a farmer in the valley. He's the one who brought Lee Trevino to El Paso from Dallas so Trevino could help him beat some of the "coyotes" in the area.

Martin had heard about Trevino's golfing through the

grapevine. Trevino wasn't well known then. Martin helped get him a job in Horizon City Country Club pro shop where Trevino would clean clubs and shine shoes for $30 a week.

I met Lettunich while playing golf at Horizon one day. We got to talking and soon began playing golf together. I played with him and Trevino many times.

The customary match would be for four or five of us to play together against Trevino. "Fat boy, get your four together," Trevino would tell me. We played for $5 a person.

The four or five of us would play our best ball against Trevino. It sounded like a pretty good deal, but it wasn't. We never beat Trevino. He'd take our money every time. But it was a lot of fun.

Lettunich and I also did a lot of hunting together.

Other supporters I got to know real well down the valley included Mike Maros and Reese Lutich.

Martin and Reese had big gardens and would invite all of us to come and pick whatever we needed. Some of us would go to the gardens with baskets and come home loaded with vegetables.

They were good times.

And let me end this chapter with a special note for one of the finest persons I've ever met, Virginia Farah.

Her son, Clifford, was a big fan of the Miners. He followed us almost everywhere we went. He was killed in an auto accident.

Mrs. Farah, on behalf of her son, set up a fund and became one of our biggest boosters, financial and otherwise. When we hold our annual basketball camp, she helps put up the out-of-town entrants. She provides both room and board.

I can't begin to express how much I admire her.

Twenty Eight

THEY NICKNAMED ME "THE BEAR." Some people have asked me how I got the nickname. I never did like it, so I'm going to let Eddie Mullens tell you in his own words how that came about:

> I came up with the nickname in the mid-1960s, even before Haskins won the national championship.
>
> He wasn't quite as big then as he is now, but he was still a big guy. He prowls around and growls a lot during a game. Because of that I hung the nickname on him of "The Bear." Not just "Bear," mind you, but *The* Bear."
>
> He got upset with me. He told me, "Aw, cut that crap out. I don't like that nickname."
>
> I told him it was too late. I had put it in my news releases and everybody was picking it up. It was being used in newspapers, radio and television and even the fans were calling him that.
>
> It's an affectionate term. Really, I wish everybody could see a picture of Don taken by El Paso photographer Brian Kanof, who worked for Guynes Printing Co. The picture shows Haskins during a game against Ohio State. Haskins is standing up and he has his hands in a grasping motion just like a bear.

Those who know Haskins or who come into contact with him think the name is appropriate.

Now, I don't want anyone to think it was a takeoff on Paul "Bear" Bryant. Maybe some people, including Haskins, thought it was. But the legendary University of Alabama football coach was known simply as Bear Bryant. Haskins is known as The Bear. No one calls him Bear Haskins. It's just, "The Bear."

Haskins, by the way, is so intense during a game that I used to say that he wouldn't recognize his own mother if she sat on the bench with him. I had that privilege right after I accepted the job at UTEP. I hadn't reported yet but I ran into Haskins while covering a game at West Texas State. He had brought the Miners up there and invited me to sit on the bench with him.

I did. During the game, he would turn around and talk to me and I could tell that he wasn't recognizing me.

I read one time where University of Arizona coach Fred Snowden said that Haskins can change the course of a game just with his presence because he is so involved and thinking so far ahead of what actions to take and what moves to make.

I don't know about all that Eddie said but I do know the nickname has stuck.

Twenty Nine

THE POST-NATE ARCHIBALD ERA in the 1970s saw some good times and some bad times.

Thanks mostly to Dick Gibbs, a six-six senior by then, we finished with a winning record of 15–10 in 1970–71. That was our first year without Archibald and we missed him something awful.

Charley Brakes, a junior, was another outstanding player that season. So were Bob Doyle, a six-three senior, and Scott English, a six-five junior.

Vandenburg had recruited English from Chatman, California and he was getting better but was still a year away from full potential.

Doyle was an excellent shot and was coming off a great season as a junior. But he had a tough time his senior year, and it took us half the season to figure out why. Archibald had been such a great penetrator that it would help Doyle get open. Without Archibald, Doyle had a hard time getting open shots.

Doyle was such a good shooter, though, that after graduation he played in Europe for several years.

We finished second in the WAC. It was the first of five second places we were to get before winning the title again in 1983. We should have won some championships those years but we had so many injuries it was unbelievable.

We had a player in the wings this 1970 season, who was to turn out to be a superstar. He was Jim Forbes, a local product out of Bel Air High School. Forbes was six feet seven and was highly recruited. I'll tell you how much talent he had. He made the United States Pan American team as a freshman and the United States Olympic team as a sophomore!

Forbes would be a millionaire today if it hadn't been for a knee injury.

He had the worst luck of any outstanding player I've ever had. He tore up a knee in his very first scrimmage his junior year. He was coming in for a layup and a teammate got in his way. Forbes tried to stop and overextended his knee. It never healed properly.

Even so, he was drafted high in the NBA draft. I still consider him one of the finest players ever to play at UTEP or anywhere else. Besides being a great player, he was a leader. I remember one game where he was hurting so bad he practically played on one knee. He hit fifteen of eighteen field goal attempts against University of Arizona although he could hardly move around.

He played well at home or away. In fact, he played even better away from home.

Because of the no-freshman rule, he didn't play with us in 1970–71. But he was to help us to winning seasons the next three years.

After graduation, he became my assistant, then went on to become a high school coach in El Paso.

Thirty

DURING THE SUMMER OF 1971 I was chosen as one of the coaches for the Olympic Development Team.

There were several coaches chosen and each had a team to work with. We would play games around the country. I met Bobby Knight that summer. He was another of the development coaches chosen.

The head coach for the entire United States Olympic baskeball program was my old coach, Henry Iba.

All this was in preparation for the 1972 Olympics.

There were some things that hurt the U.S. team about that time. Bill Walton, one of the greatest players of all time at UCLA, didn't participate. He didn't give a reason; he just said he didn't want to join.

There was also a lot of racial turmoil at that time. There were a couple of athletes at the Olympic camp who wouldn't stand for the National Anthem.

Coaches select their own Olympic teams now, but they didn't then. There was a selection committee who did the picking.

So a lot of good players weren't selected or didn't play because of attitudes.

As everyone knows, Russia beat us in a very controversial game in the 1972 Olympics. I was Iba's assistant coach.

I hate to talk about it even now. The language barrier had something to do with it but any way you look at it, it was plain robbery.

The game was over and we had won and they put time back on the clock. They did that three times.

Finally, Russia scored and won the game by a point.

That night, officials said, no, that we had won the game. Then they had another meeting. They went back and forth.

There was a panel of five Olympic officials. Those from Communist countries would vote for Russia. Those not from Communist countries would vote for us.

We left there about three in the morning. The last thing I heard was that the panel had voted that we won. Then at 5:00 A.M. the decision was changed again.

The worst thing about the whole game was that the officials to this date have not signed the book. For a game to be official, it must be signed by the referees.

Two officials wrote letters later saying that the game had been over and they couldn't sign the book. I got one of those letters.

Coaches don't get medals in the Olympics, only athletes. But our players refused to accept any.

I got to know Bobby Knight pretty well during the 1971 Olympic Development year and we became friends. He's one heck of a good guy. Oh, he gets into scraps with the media. I've tried to talk to him about that but he just hates the press.

There was an incident in El Paso which illustrates some of his problems. He brought a team to play UTEP in 1985. He was interviewed by a sports writer on the *El Paso Herald-Post*. Knight uses colorful language when he speaks. The sports writer put one of his bad words in the paper and it caused quite a stir. Knight didn't mean anything; he was just kidding around. He never dreamed the bad word would be printed.

We've been fishing and hunting together several times. He's friendly and fun to be with. He's also very helpful. He goes out of his way to help his players in time of need and helps other coaches with any type of problem.

He's an outstanding individual.

Thirty One

WITH JIM FORBES IN THE LINEUP as a sophomore, we won twenty-one games and lost only seven during the 1971–72 season.

Besides Forbes, we had Brakes and English back plus a couple of fine young players in Beto Bautista and Gus Bailey.

Bautista and Bailey, like Forbes, were also local products. Bautista came out of Austin High School and Bailey out of Burges High School.

English had an outstanding season. He averaged 16.4 points per game, hitting .51 percent from the floor and .75 percent from the free throw line. Forbes, despite his youth, averaged 13.8 and Brakes, 11.6.

I loved Bautista. He is one of the greatest hustlers I've ever coached.

114

It's strange how I got Bautista to come to UTEP. He was so small, five-nine, that he wasn't highly recruited. But there was another player on his high school team who was being scouted by a lot of coaches, including me. His name was Gave Nava.

Nava was outstanding but the more I went to scout him the more interested I became in Bautista.

Nava wound up at University of New Mexico, where he had an outstanding career. But not one single time when we played New Mexico did Nava get the better of Bautista.

Nava was a fine young man in addition to being a great player. He was killed in a tragic freak accident a few years after his graduation from New Mexico.

Bautista had one of the biggest hearts I've ever seen in a player. But there was one incident that bothered him.

We lost the WAC title by half a game that 1971–72 season when we got beat in double overtime by Brigham Young University. Bautista missed a late free throw that would have won the game for us. He had been an excellent free throw shooter and, in fact, had kept us in this particular game with five or six earlier free throws.

But he was devastated by the one he missed and he was never a good free throw shooter again.

The missed free throw wasn't the end of the world. Things like that happen, and remember, he was only a sophomore that season.

I told him to forget about it.

"Coach, I'd like to," he told me, "but three hundred thousand Mexicans won't let me."

He was referring to the ribbing he took from the large Hispanic community in El Paso. Bautista was of Mexican descent himself, of course, and he was joking when he said that. But you could tell he was hurting.

Bautista and Bailey complimented each other well. Bautista was a penetrator and he and Bailey worked off each other. Also, both were such great defensive players that in my estimation I had the two strongest defensive guards west of the Mississippi.

I still think we would have gone far if we had been chosen for the NCAA play-offs. But our fine 21–7 record was passed over.

We did go to the NIT in New York but got beat by Niagara 76–57.

Thirty Two

THERE WAS AN UNSAVORY INCIDENT the next year, the 1972–73 season.

We had a player who was a straight A student. It never came out in the media, but I found he had been not only using drugs, but selling them.

I found out about it when one of the other players came up to me and said, "Coach, why are you putting up with this?"

I said, "What do you mean?"

Then he told me.

I hadn't paid much attention to the player in question, who I won't name, because he wasn't very good.

We were on a game trip at the time. I went to his room and found the stuff. I confiscated it and sent it to his father.

In fact, I sent both the stuff and the player to the father along with a note. I told the player never to come back, not even to get his clothes.

What a different type he was from my other players.

One fine young man that season was Frank Keton, who I had recruited from Coronado High School in El Paso. He is one of the best shooters I've ever had. Against Indiana University that season he hit on eight of eight field goal attempts. And he was just a sophomore.

He was a person of character, on and off the court. And it carried on into his life. He became a successful business-man and highly respected in the community.

He didn't finish his basketball career. He was never all that high on basketball. He played mostly because his father wanted him to.

His dad died when he was a junior. Two weeks after his father's death, Frank came into my office. I knew right away what he was going to tell me. He said he didn't want to play anymore. I understood and said okay.

Ed Lynum and Rudy Alvarez were other outstanding young men from El Paso. I've been accused of not recruiting local talent but when it's been there I've gone after it. Look at all the El Paso players we had around this time: Forbes, Bautista, Lynum, Keton, Bailey and Alvarez.

We finished the season with a 16–10 record. We finished strong, beating Utah 64–54, Wyoming by exactly the same score, Colorado State 62–44 and New Mexico 63–60.

But it was too late to get a post-season bid.

We had a freshman that year who was to turn out one of my best players ever. His name: Gary Brewster.

Incidentally, the president of the college up to this time had been Dr. Joseph R. Smiley, a nationally recognized authority in education administration.

I never met him. He was president four years and not one time was I called to his office nor did I run into him to talk to him. Even to this day I have not met him.

He would write me a letter after a big game and congratulate us, but that was it.

Everyone says he was a nice man, and I'm sure he was.

Thirty Three

WE WENT INTO THE 1973–74 SEASON with high hopes. We had Forbes, Brewster, Bailey, Bautista, Lynum and Alvarez returning.

In addition, freshmen had become eligible to play by this time and we had a good one in the fold. His name was Ron Jones.

A key player was Brewster, who was now a sophomore.

Brewster was highly sought after but he didn't want to go far away from home. He was from Midland, Texas.

We were lucky to get Jones. He and another player from Shortridge High School in Indianapolis came to UTEP for a visit. We were really trying to recruit the other player but he decided to go to University of Washington. Their coach was trying to get both of them to go to the same school as a package deal. Jones signed with us.

I got the best of that deal. Jones was a tough nut. We're talking here about another hard-nosed kid like Bautista. They were cut from the same mold.

Another surprise this season was Jake Poole. I never did understand why he didn't start at Burges High School in El Paso. He was a great shooter and turned out to be All-WAC his senior year.

Brewster was a fantastic defensive player. I rank him with Nolan Richardson, Andy Stoglin, Jim Forbes and Beto Bautista among my all-time best defensive players. Whoever I put Brewster on to guard, he would dominate. He was six feet eight but could guard a center, forward or guard just as easily. He was like Forbes in that respect.

Brewster started every game for us as a freshman and averaged 11.8 points per game. He was selected to the Sun Carnival Tournament all-tourney team and also Most Valuable Player. And he received honorable mention on the All-WAC team.

As a sophomore that season, he started every game, too. He would gain even more honors in years to come, just like he had in high school.

In high school, he was the top vote-getter on the 4A All-State team and was also named honorable mention All-America while averaging 24.2 points for Midland High School.

We wound up with a record of eighteen victories and seven losses.

It was a tough WAC race that year. University of New

Mexico won it but lost four games. The Lobos had a 10–4 record. We were 8–6, two games behind.

Thirty Four

THE NEXT SEASON, 1974–75, we moved up to a 10–4 record in WAC play, good for second place, and had an overall record of 20–6.

Arizona State won the WAC championship. The Sun Devils beat us the first time we met 61–56 but we beat them 75–70 in our second meeting.

We finished second three times in the WAC between 1971 and 1976. Either Forbes or Brewster was injured during those second-place seasons.

Brewster hurt his back during the summer. He was on some construction job and was hurt lifting two doors at the same time. That's the way he was, always trying to do things in twos.

Forbes was gone by this time but Brewster stepped into his position nicely despite the injury.

Ron Jones was a sophomore and getting to be a big help.

Brewster averaged 15.4 points during the season and 14.8 in WAC play despite the fact he was hurt and was primarily a defensive player. Poole kept surprising and wound up our second leading scorer with an average of 8.5.

We had a really well-balanced team and a lot of players saw action. That included Ed Lynum, John Saffle, Tom Paul, Charles Draper, Rudy Alvarez and Calvin Hale.

We had some good wins in addition to our victory over Arizona State. That season we beat Creighton, Miami of Ohio, Texas A&M and all WAC teams at least once.

We got into the NCAA tournament and went up against Indiana University and Coach Bobby Knight.

Indiana had a great team and should have won the national title. They beat us 78–53 but it wasn't as lopsided as the score would indicate. We were down only three points at the half. Towards the end of a game I usually let everybody play if the game is out of reach or if we're way ahead. I put in a lot of substitutes and Indiana scored a lot of points toward the end.

Indiana had a score to settle. We had beaten Indiana a couple of seasons before 74–65.

One incident stands out very well in my mind about that 1975 game. One of Indiana's top players ran into Ron Jones right in the middle of the floor with about thirty seconds to go in the half. He just plain ran over Jones.

They called the foul on my player. It was Jones' third foul of the game and it really hurt us in the second half.

Thirty Five

OUR LAST WINNING SEASON for a while was to come in 1975–76. We went 20–7. It was my sixth twenty-win season at UTEP up to this point.

Brewster was a senior and he was a marvel to watch. Whenever we played somebody it was like we were playing against four men. Whoever we put Brewster on wouldn't get anything.

Things were beginning to get tough in recruiting, though. We were still in little Memorial Gym and other schools were taking players away from us because of it.

We knew we would be in trouble when Brewster would graduate. Players like him are hard to find. Not only was he an influence with his athletic ability, but with his determination. We couldn't lose with him. He wouldn't let us.

Calvin Hale, a six feet six player we had recruited from Detroit, was on the squad this season. He was just a sophomore but showed great promise.

Incidentally, Calvin's mother has to be one of the all-time great basketball parents. Her name is Dorothy. She would come down to see her son play often and she would visit with me. She still comes to El Paso. Her daughter, Beverly, came down with her mother from Detroit to see Calvin play one day and never left. She got a job with the local telephone company and is still living in El Paso.

We still get to see Dorothy because she comes to visit her daughter.

Calvin is now living in Houston.

Another good player that year was Tom "Gator" Pauling. Nate Archibald sent him to us from the playgrounds of New York. Gator hated school. He was a fun lover. But he worked hard on the court and was fun to watch. He had long arms and could really jump. He was six-five.

John Saffle, a six-eight player from Irving, Texas, came into his own as a senior. He shot over sixty percent from the field this season, which is one of the reasons we did so well.

This was a strange team in a way. It was almost like they didn't like each other. We'd go to the airport and there'd be one guy here and another one over there. On my other teams, players got in little groups of two, three or four and talked. Not these guys.

They wouldn't even eat together. It was weird.

But they kept winning, so I didn't do anything about it.

We had a frustrating end to an otherwise fine season. Here's how it went in our last three games:

We nipped Brigham Young University 51–50 then we beat Utah 81–71. But in the final game of the season New Mexico beat us 59–58.

We finished second in the WAC again.

What really hurt was that we had beaten New Mexico earlier in the year.

Thirty Six

DR. ARLEIGH TEMPLETON HAD ANNOUNCED in July of 1973 the plans for the Special Events Center. It was to be built on an area occupied by a practice football field. The site would require excavation into hills. There would be seating for between 12,000 and 13,000 spectators. Underneath one end would be the dressing rooms and offices, including mine.

It was completed midway through the 1976–77 basketball season.

We were without Brewster now but we got off to a good start. We won ten of our first fourteen games, beating such teams as University of Colorado, New Mexico State and Baylor.

Then we moved into the Special Events Center. What we had thought would be a good luck charm turned out to be anything but that.

Oh, the Special Events Center is beautiful. Big and spacious and a handsome structure.

We proceeded to lose eleven of our next twelve games.

We were very small. Pauling was our tallest player at six-five. Poole and Jones were only six-one. They were our leaders. On top of that, we had no depth.

I still say that if we had finished the season at Memorial

Gym and not gone to the Special Events Center for our last five home games to make a few extra dollars we would have had a winning season.

We got Jones and Pauling hurt just before we moved into the Special Events Center. It happened during the last two minutes against Brigham Young. We won 64–62 but it was costly.

Our first game in the Special Events Center was against Wyoming. There we were with two of our top players hurt, no height, no depth and a young team.

The kids tried. In fact, they tried too hard. The house was packed and they were trying to make a good impression. Wyoming beat us 62–59.

It was a heartbreaker. And there were to be more of them.

Colorado State beat us next 51–46. We went on the road for two games then came back and lost at the Special Events Center to New Mexico 59–58, Utah 66–65 and Brigham Young 65–63.

We lost all five games at the Special Events Center by a total of eleven points with the biggest margin being five points.

Some people said the Special Events Center was a jinx. If you call getting two of our top players hurt a jinx, okay.

If it was, it was to continue for two more years. That was my first losing season as a coach at any level — and there were to be two more of them.

Thirty Seven

WE WENT 10–16 in 1977–78 and 11–15 in 1978–79.

I had decided to go the freshman route. Looking back on it now maybe I should have got some junior college transfers. But I didn't, and I blame myself for letting those losing seasons happen. Now I feel like I threw our freshmen to the wolves.

They were fun seasons despite all the losses, though. I mean, the players I had were young and scrappy and gave it their all. We lost a bunch of games by one or two points.

Actually, I did have one junior college transfer but he wasn't with us long. I won't tell his name but he was six feet six and an outstanding all-around player. I have no doubt we would have wound up on the plus side if we could have kept him. But a problem arose.

It didn't take him long to realize how important he was to the team. He saw all the inexperienced freshmen making mistakes.

He came to me one day and tried to put the bite on me. He told me his mother needed a coat. I told him, "Okay, go home and work to get her one." He went.

Our freshmen during the 1977–78 season were Roshern Amie, six-seven from Marshall, Texas; Jim Bowden, six-three from El Paso Burges High School; Anthony Burns, six-seven from Marshall, Texas; Tim Crenshaw, six-four from El Paso Eastwood High School; Earl Fuller, five-nine from Brooklyn, New York; Darold Molix, six-seven from El Paso Eastwood, and Steve Yellen, five-eleven from Frishkill, New York.

They were still inexperienced the following year. And we had picked up other freshmen. Joining us in 1978–79 were Terry White, six-nine from El Paso Eastwood; Mike McDuffen, six-four from Detroit, and Oscar Alvarado, six-five from El Paso High School.

Maybe some people were disappointed in our losing seasons but the reaction wasn't really too bad. I came to gain a lot of admiration for fans and the El Paso media during those years. They stuck with us and there was really very little negative publicity.

I think I know why. People liked the scrappiness of these kids. They weren't quitters. I've always said that if you give it your all and never quit people will stay with you.

Oh, attendance fell a little, but not all that much. People can tell if a team is trying. If the players quit, then their fans should quit. That didn't happen.

Not only were the players not quitters, they were fine young men who never griped about anything.

Which reminds me of an incident that happened off the court. The Marshall, Texas kids — Amie and Burns — came up to me one day while they were still freshmen.

They said, "Coach, could you move Sunday practice so we can go to church on Sunday?"

They were very sincere. They were both devout Baptists.

They stood there for a while. I knew they wanted to say something else. Finally, Burns said, "Coach, we really like you but we think you cuss too much."

127

I was taken aback for a moment, but then I told them I would try to tone the cussing down.

I guess I got a little sermon from them, and they must have had some impact on me. I had been awfully profane. I stopped and thought about it. I toned down some, although some of my recent players may wonder about that.

Despite the problems we had in the Special Events Center — three losing seasons our first three years — the new gym was beginning to pay off in recruiting. And winning seasons would return.

Thirty Eight

BEFORE I GO INTO RECOUNTING our experiences in the 1980s, let me tell you about a couple of incidents that occurred before then.

When Archibald was going into his senior year in 1969, I was offered the job of head basketball coach at University of Detroit.

Detroit officials had called me three or four times and I told them each time I wasn't interested. But they kept on calling and I finally said I'd go up and talk to them.

One of the fellows on the selection committee owned a big apartment complex. He had a big table in a conference room there and he and the other members sat and talked to me. All of them were pretty young but were interested in the program. Bob Callahan, who had been the basketball coach there for twenty years, had been retired and named athletic director.

The job didn't really appeal to me but I wasn't making much money and I didn't think there would be any harm in listening.

The fellows there asked me to write on a piece of paper how much it would take for me to take the job. I tripled what I was making at UTEP and handed the paper to them, thinking they would turn me down.

They looked at the paper and said "fine."

The figure I had put down — $60,000 — didn't include membership to country clubs, two cars, radio and television shows and so on.

The whole package would have come to around $100,000 and remember, that was nearly twenty years ago.

I started to add things to the deal, trying to make it even harder on them. They told me they would build me a house. They took me out to a subdivision by a lake. The site was beautiful.

I called my wife in El Paso and told her I was taking the job. She couldn't believe I was making that decision.

But by now I was sort of trapped. They kept saying "yes" to everything I asked.

All of a sudden I found myself surrounded by these people and all those goodies dangling in front of me and the papers ready for me to sign.

I went ahead and signed.

The next day there was a press conference. I had questions thrown at me like "What's it like out in the desert?" and "Are there many snakes?" and "How about all those Mexicans?"

I'd never had exposure to any questions like that. I didn't know what to answer. And it wasn't just one person asking questions like that. It was the whole damn bunch.

I didn't like that one bit. I'd been exposed to sportswriters in the Southwest like Bob Ingram, Chuck Whitlock and the man who helped me with this book, Ray Sanchez. They had some tact.

Another thing that upset me very much was when one fellow took me over to what was to be my office. It was Callahan's old office, and it was a grand place. I'd had a little cubbyhole at Memorial Gym.

They told me they were moving Callahan "down the hall." I thought to myself, "Here this man has given twenty years of his life to this school and they're treating him like this. What's to keep them from treating me the same way someday?"

All of a sudden you find that money doesn't mean that much and that you'd rather be where people treat you right.

Oh, yes. Another subject that came up was our 1966 championship team. The Detroit media kept referring to the players as "outlaws." They wanted to know what the "outlaws" were doing now. That really burned me, knowing that my players had all been fine young men.

They never attacked me personally. I think there was a split in the town with some people supporting Callahan and others against him. I guess those who supported Callahan took their frustration out on me.

Anyway, I didn't like the whole set up. I called El Paso and asked if I could have my job back. I was told yes.

I was a coach at Detroit for exactly one day. I've never had any regrets not taking the job, although I sure liked one player at Detroit.

His name was Spencer Haywood, who had the greatest

talent any coach could wish for. He would have been a junior the next season. He went on to a great career in the NBA.

Thirty Nine

THE OTHER INCIDENT occurred in 1970.

Eddie Mullens, my assistants and I were sitting in a restaurant in Laramie, Wyoming having dinner. We were there to play University of Wyoming the next night.

A lady came over and introduced herself. She said she hated Bill Strannigan, the Wyoming basketball coach. I didn't know it then, but I heard later that this lady had a crush on Strannigan, who was single at the time, and that she was after him but he wouldn't give her a tumble.

Anyway, she told me she had a voodoo doll. She said she stuck a pin in it every night. We all laughed, but she went on. She asked me if I would like to beat Wyoming the next night. Of course, I said yes.

She told me to give her a strand off my coat, or any of my garments. We thought it was a great joke and were laughing but I reached over and took a little strand off the sleeve of my coat. I didn't want to ruin the coat by taking too big a piece.

She looked at the strand and said, "I guess you want it to be a close game."

I answered, "No, I'd like to win by a comfortable margin. Something like ten points."

She said, "Okay. The score will be 80 to 70."

I took a longer strand off my coat and gave it to her. She put it in a paper napkin and took it home with her.

We were still laughing when she left.

I mentioned the incident to Strannigan. He said he'd heard about a Voodoo Lady who stuck pins in dolls. I've always been a little superstitious and apparently he was, too.

The game came up and we got ahead. I forgot all about the "voodoo" incident in the heat of the game. I looked up at the scoreboard near the end of the game and saw we were ahead by twelve points. Then I remembered.

The score was 80 to 68 and there was only one second to go. One of the Wyoming players got off a shot just as the buzzer ending the game went off. The ball hit the backboard and banked off it — right into the net.

The final score was UTEP 80, Wyoming 70, just like the lady had said.

I went to see Strannigan after the game. "Damn, that's the worst thing I've ever seen," he said.

The next year, Strannigan called me before we went to Laramie to play his team again. I knew what he wanted to ask me but he wouldn't say anything about it. He just talked and talked.

Finally, he asked me what time we were getting into Laramie. I told him I didn't know, that we would get there the day before the game because we had a few things to do.

That did it. "Haskins, you're going to go see that Voodoo Lady, aren't you?" he asked.

I said, "Yeah, I am."

After we got there he wanted me to tell him how much

we were going to beat him by. I told him I couldn't tell him this time.

This went on for about four years and he couldn't beat us during that time. He was going downright crazy.

Actually, though, the Voodoo Lady met us only two more years. When she stopped coming to see me, then it was my turn to go crazy. I kept looking for her.

Of course, I wasn't about to tell Strannigan she had stopped seeing me. He would call me and ask me if I was going to see the Voodoo Lady. "Oh, yeah," I would reply.

About fifteen years later, she sent me a letter and explained why she quit meeting me. She said she stopped the voodoo stuff because Strannigan was to be replaced as head coach. She said she had nothing against University of Wyoming and, in fact, that she like Wyoming very much. She just hadn't liked Strannigan.

Some people consider her calling the score and our winning all those games a coincidence. But I got to asking around Laramie and found the people there believe she had these powers. They told me she had won a car and all sorts of other prizes in raffles.

One guy told me, "This lady is really spooky."

I said, "Tell me about it."

Forty

THE 1980s GOT OFF ON A GOOD NOTE, and stayed on a good note for years.

The scrappy young players that had two losing seasons in a row were juniors in the 1979–80 season. They'd gotten older, and if anyone had claimed I was getting old, like they did about Darrell Royal, then I must have gotten younger.

Anyway, we won twenty games and lost only eight.

If there had been a Special Events Center jinx, which I never believed, it was broken.

We were invited to the NIT and although we had to play both games on the road we upset an outstanding Wichita team 58–56 before losing to University of Michigan 74–65.

Games we had lost by a point or two while the kids were freshmen and sophomores we won this season.

Jim Bowden (we all called him Jimbo) was one of the few seniors. He was a fine player and a steadying influence.

Roshern Amie was a junior and came of age on the court. So did Anthony Burns.

Tim Crenshaw was a home-grown product and he was very popular, just like Bowden. Crenshaw was sort of an in-between player. He wasn't quite big enough to play inside and was a step slow to play outside but he was a hustler.

Incidentally, this was a smart group of players. Nearly all

of them were excellent students. Crenshaw graduated in just three-and-a-half years. He's in the banking business and doing great.

So is Bowden. He's a dentist.

Arriving on the team was Terry White, a six feet nine, 220-pounder from El Paso's Eastwood High School. He was just a sophomore in 1980 but saw a lot of action and was a big help on the boards. He would develop later into one of the finest rebounders I've ever coached.

Another young player who helped us and would develop into a superstar was a freshman we had recruited out of Jones High School in Houston. He was six feet five then and had been selected to the Texas Blue Chip list. He had been all-district, all-city and all-state and had been highly recruited. His name was Fred Reynolds.

We got Reynolds as part of a package with Rick Thompson, a six-six player who was being recruited as one of the top five players in Texas. But Thompson wasn't with our basketball team very long. He was more interested in track, and joined our track team. He was a great high jumper. He cleared seven feet seven.

That year we brought in one junior college transfer, Julius Wayne, who was to be a big asset at guard. He was only six feet one but he was a great athlete and a good leaper. We got him from Compton College. He's been playing basketball in Europe for many years.

Another guard on the team was Steve Yellen, a junior. He was awfully small, only five feet eleven, but he had a lot of heart and always gave you his best.

One of the most exciting games in my career occurred that season when we beat University of New Mexico 68–67. Here's how our sports information director, Eddie Mullens, chronicled that game:

Albuquerque has always been a tough place to play and this February night at the sold out "Pit" was a nightmare for the Miners . . .

The Lobos were still suffering through a scandal called "Lobogate" that ruined its basketball program. However, the Lobos were still competitive as long as star guard Kenny Page was shooting the ball. Page proceeded to shoot the lights out in the first half against the Miners, hitting his first twelve field goal attempts, and New Mexico raced out to a twenty-point lead midway in the first half.

During the second half Don Haskins sent his club right after Kenny Page. Haskins utilized every pressing defense he could think of to get Page stopped . . .

The Lobos wilted against UTEP's pressure defense, leading to numerous turnovers. UTEP rallied thanks to its great defensive play and won the game on a twenty-five-foot buzzer shot by Miner forward Anthony Burns.

I dont know if it was the defensive changes I made that worked or if Page just cooled off but it's a game I'll never forget.

Fred Reynolds was one of the smoothest players ever to wear a UTEP uniform. He's going for two points in this photo.

Jeep Jackson, Quintan Gates and Donnell Allen (left to right) have fun during a scrimmage. Jackson and Gates were with the Miners during their entire five-year WAC reign.

Juden Smith is rated one of the best all-around athletes ever to play for Haskins. He's shown in action against BYU's Bob Capener.

Dave Feitl (No. 33) was a big man for the Miners in the 1980s. He was drafted by the Houston Rockets of the NBA.

Wayne "Soup" Campbell overcame an injury to help the Miners win their fifth straight WAC basketball championship.

Forty One

TO SHOW THEIR FINE SEASON wasn't a fluke, those juniors came right back with another winning season in 1980–81 as seniors.

We played a lot of games that season, but we won eighteen of them and lost twelve.

The young players we had been picking up helped, but it was really those young players who had suffered through two losing seasons who deserve the credit. They came through time and again as juniors and seniors.

I can't begin to express how proud I am of them. They'll always hold a special place in my heart.

They finished second in the WAC in 1979–80 but the best they could do in 1980–81 was finish fourth, although with a winning conference record of 9–7. University of Utah was loaded that season and ran away with the title. We played them close but couldn't beat 'em. Utah beat us 69–65 and 69–59.

Wyoming also beat us in a couple of thrillers, 44–42 and 63–58. Oh, how I could have used that Voodoo Lady then.

We did have some good games including some against non-conference teams. We beat Nevada-Las Vegas 85–77 and lost a nail-biter to a strong Villanova team 43–41.

We picked up a player that season who was to become

141

one of the most subtly effective players I've ever coached. His name is Paul Cunningham.

He was six feet six and looked like a sort of easy-going guy. His easy manner was an illusion.

He didn't post good statistics. I mean, he wasn't a leading scorer or a leading rebounder. He was one of those types that when you look at the film after a game you're surprised at how effective he had been.

He'd knock down a ball and make a steal or deflect a pass or grab a crucial rebound. He just made things happen. And he was everywhere on defense.

You'd look at the newspaper the next day and see that he had scored only seven points. And you knew that didn't begin to tell the story of what a great influence he had been.

Cunningham was recruited out of Houston. He was to be one of several Houston players who would help us continue our winning ways in the 1980s.

Another freshman that 1980–81 season was Anthony Bailey. He was a stocky kid, standing six feet even and weighing close to two hundred pounds.

Bailey was a guard and a pretty good shot. His nickname in high school was "St. Anthony" and it stuck with him through his career with the Miners. He was often referred to simply as "The Saint."

I don't know if some fans considered that a bit out of taste, but the way I see it, a little help from above never hurts.

Forty Two

THE NEXT YEAR (the 1981–82 season) saw the greatest crop of freshmen I'd ever had. Not necessarily individually, but as a group.

Because of red-shirting, some of them stayed at UTEP five years. They finished second in the WAC in 1981–82 then either won the title outright or tied for it four straight years! That, of course, is a conference record.

All of these freshmen were recruited by Tim Floyd. Here they are:

—David Feitl, six-eleven from Tucson.
—Luster Goodwin, six feet even from Houston.
—Kent Lockhart, six-four from Palo Alto, California.
—Juden Smith, six-six from New Orleans.
—Don Bronson, six-seven from Lufkin, Texas.

Feitl, Goodwin, Lockhart and Smith earned all kinds of WAC honors.

Lockhart had been quite a star in high school and was sought after so much I told Floyd not to go after him. But then Floyd found out that Lockhart's grandparents lived in El Paso. That gave us an opening.

Floyd went and talked to his grandparents and brought the grandfather out to our school. The grandfather got so he would drop by the school now and then.

I finally went out to sign Lockhart myself. I didn't have to. Floyd had already sold him on UTEP.

Same way with Feitl. Floyd had him signed before I even met him. I've got to rank Floyd among the top five recruiters in the nation. I don't think I could do the things he's done.

Lockhart turned out to be one of the hardest workers I've ever had, and so did Feitl, Smith and Goodwin. I've always said that the players who work hard in practice work hard during a game, and these fellows proved it. Good players are good practicers.

Feitl got hurt his freshman year and I red-shirted him. But Terry White was a senior now and he filled our big-man needs.

Also, Fred Reynolds came into his own as a junior and had a great season. Paul Cunningham was a sophomore and seeing a lot of action.

We brought in a junior college transfer from Mesa Junior College in Arizona by the name of Byron Walker. He was only five-ten but a heck of a guard. He was our playmaker and did a great job of setting up plays.

The only other senior on the team besides White was Virgil Kennedy, a six-six guard from Dayton, Ohio.

The team won twenty games and lost only eight during the season and was 11–5 in WAC play. Wyoming wound up as the WAC champion but we beat them both times we played, 51–45 the first time and 43–37 the second time. The scores were low because we both had great defenses, not because either team held the ball.

Although we didn't win the conference title I was absolutely sure we would get an NCAA bid because of our fine record and the fact we beat the WAC champion twice. It didn't happen. And not only that, we didn't even get a bid to the NIT. Our team really got robbed.

A lot of blame for our not getting an NIT bid was put on our athletic director, Ed Swartz. But it was my fault. I had been so sure we would get an NCAA bid that I told him not to mess with the NIT.

He would come up to me and say, "I need to be calling the NIT." And I would tell him I didn't want him to.

He followed my advice, then got all the heat for not putting pressure on the NIT selection committee to pick us.

I told everybody it was my fault but no one would listen.

I feel bad about that to this day.

Forty Three

WHILE ON THE SUBJECT of controversy, let me say something about our public address announcer for many years, Paul Strelzin.

To some, Paul was controversial but to me and my team he was an asset. A major asset.

He was not only a good announcer, with a voice that carries well in any crowd, but he added a lot of color and excitement to the game. He would get the fans into the action with his hollering and whooping.

He probably started a trend around the Southwest if not around the country. Some people at our school worried about his going overboard. But I'd take our team to other places and the public address announcer there would do the same as Strelzin. When we go to "The Pit" at University of New Mexico, for example, we get hollered at, too.

Strelzin would use nicknames for all the players, whether they were given to them by Strelzin or Eddie Mullens or had them before they came to UTEP, and the players liked that. Players like to be recognized as something special.

Some of those members of that great crop of freshmen I talked about were often known as much by their nicknames as by their real names. For instance:

Dave Feitl became known as "The Cheez."

Juden Smith became known as "The Beast."

Ken Lockhart became known as "La Machine."

Luster Goodwin became known as "Pony."

All of them, at one time or another, made All-WAC and were extremely exciting to watch. Whenever they scored, Strelzin would holler out their nicknames and the crowd would go wild.

Another of Strelzin's trademarks was that whenever we got the ball on an out-of-bounds call he would holler "MMMMMMMiner ball." He would hold the "M" for a long time as the crowd went into a frenzy.

We got a player in 1982 who was a natural for Strelzin to put a tag on. He was Wayne Campbell, a six-seven forward from New Orleans. What would be more appropriate than "Soup?"

Strelzin did a great job and I miss him.

Forty Four

ONE OF THE BIGGEST PLEASURES I've derived from coaching the Miners has been the coverage of the El Paso media. We've had very little negative press.

That's not true about just any other place. Even up the road at New Mexico State there have been a lot of negative things written.

Some coaches get so they don't want the press to come to their practices. They'll have closed practices. I know that the idea of "closed practices" is not because of the public. It's to keep the press out.

I've never had a closed practice and never had to bar the press from any of my workouts.

Now once in a while public workouts can get out of hand. But it's not because of the press. We used to practice at night at Memorial Gym and we would get as many as 300 people. There would be kids running around all over the place, and that can be pretty distracting. We tried to discourage some of that but it had nothing to do with the media.

Because of the good press we've received, the city has been behind us. If fans like a team it comes from the things they read or hear. The media has a lot more influence than people realize.

If newspapermen write that the previous year a team didn't

147

play up to its potential, pretty soon everybody else will be saying that, too.

Most of the things we have had in the media in El Paso have been put in a positive way.

I think that's the way college sports should be covered. And also young players like those with the El Paso Diablos minor league baseball team. Some of them are just nineteen years old and trying to make their way up the ladder.

Now if it's a player in the National Football League, the National Basketball Association or the Major Leagues, that's another matter.

Those players are professionals and getting big bucks. If they don't perform, they should be criticized.

Severe criticism at an early age can not only hurt a team but hurt a young player's career.

I think the El Paso media deserves a pat on the back for recognizing this fact.

Forty Five

THE 1982–83 TEAM RANKS as one of my favorites. We had some key injuries and floundered for a while. The team could have quit and folded but it didn't.

As a result we won the first of our five consecutive WAC championships or co-championships. We finished tied for first with University of Utah and Brigham Young University with a record of 11–5.

Overall, our record was nineteen wins and ten losses.

Byron Walker, the guard we had picked up from Mesa Junior College, was our leader. He had never played high school basketball but he developed into one of my best playmakers.

And was he tough. He's the kind of guy who if you're in a war and in a foxhole you want sitting right there next to you.

When I went to recruit him at Mesa Junior College he told me he didn't want to go to any school where he was going to lose.

He played for a heck of a coach at Mesa Junior College. His name is Tom Bennett. It's the breaks of the game that he's not a major college coach. He deserves to be.

Kevin Hamilton came on the scene that year. He was another winner. He was six feet six, weighed 210 pounds and was a tough competitor from the word go. We got him out of Los Angeles, where his team lost only seven games in three years.

Quintan Gates, a teammate of Hamilton's at Crenshaw High School in Los Angeles, also joined us that year. However, he wasn't ready to play because he suffered an injury and we red-shirted him. The injury was a knee stress fracture he incurred as a junior in high school. It had required an operation.

He was six feet seven and had long arms. He was awfully thin and fragile but he moved well and turned in several super performances for us.

We might have done even better than 19–10 but for a couple of injuries to two of our outstanding starters.

Fred Reynolds and Juden Smith both got hurt. Smith

149

played a great game against New Mexico State and we won 60–55. But he got hurt right after that and we had to red-shirt him for the season.

We met New Mexico State again a couple of weeks later and this time Reynolds got hurt. We had New Mexico State beaten but with Reynolds out our players panicked some and we lost 76–73.

We had a hard time for a while after that. When you lose two starters early in the season you can survive, but it isn't easy.

Paul Cunningham stepped in to fill some of the void and that helped.

Donnell Allen, a six-seven player, also aided us a lot. He had transferred from Jackson, Mississippi.

Reynolds' injury was a tissue tear below the knee and it took a long time to heal. He sat out the season but he was such an outstanding player that he made our Pan American team that summer.

We would have won the championship outright that season if it hadn't been for University of Hawaii. They beat us 56–55 in our first encounter. Then in the final game of the season, they beat us 62–61. We would have won that second encounter but some time was knocked off the clock and they scored late.

There were two outstanding games by my players that season. One was when we beat Brigham Young University 65–49 in Provo. That's about as fine a game as I have ever had played for me.

The other was a 68–66 win over San Diego State. Michael Cage had a tremendous game against us and we were behind by ten points with three minutes to go.

Eric Alexander, a five-nine senior guard, came off the

bench to play a key role defensively. We outscored the Aztecs 14–2 over the last three minutes to win.

We got into the NIT but had the misfortune of having to go to Fresno State to play. We played as well as we could but they beat us 71–64. It was even closer than that. We had to foul towards the end to try to get the ball and they scored to make it a seven-point edge.

Fresno State went on to win the NIT championship.

Incidentally, I became a "sportswriter" for a few days after our season. The *El Paso Herald-Post* asked me if I would give my analysis of the NCAA Final Four tournament which was to be held in Albuquerque. Derry Eads of the *Herald-Post*, who covers the Miners, helped me out. He and I would talk after the game then he would put the story in readable form and send it to the paper.

Everything went fine until the final game. The *Herald-Post* had two seats assigned to it on the press row, one for Eads and the other for Ray Sanchez. Ray didn't go so I used his pass and sat in his seat.

The NCAA decided I wasn't a sportswriter and made me move. It was no big deal. I went up into the stands and Derry and I still got our story.

I did pick the winner in my prediction before the tournament. I felt North Carolina State had everything to win and nothing to lose. Houston and Louisville were the favorites, but when you get in an NCAA tournament you may not be at your best. And they weren't. Sure enough, North Carolina State won.

Forty Six

THE 1983–84 SEASON RANKS as one of our best on a won-lost basis. We finished with twenty-seven victories and only four losses.

And we were undisputed champions of the WAC with a mark of 13–3.

We beat some good teams outside the WAC. We defeated Indiana University 65–61, Arizona State 60–55, Michigan 72–71 and University of Arizona 51–49. The win over Arizona was in overtime. It was our second overtime game of the season. Earlier, we had beaten our nearby rival, New Mexico State, 60–59 in *two* overtimes.

There were two key games in the conference race. The first one came at The Pit in Albuquerque against the University of New Mexico Lobos.

The Lobos were well ahead of us with about eleven minutes to go. Then Juden Smith, one of the best all-around athletes ever to play at UTEP, went to work. He was a terror on defense, dominated the offensive boards and scored eleven of his thirteen points in the last eleven minutes of the game.

With ten seconds to go, the Lobos' Tim Garrett scored on a reverse lay-up to give New Mexico the lead at 59–58. Luster Goodwin took our in-bound pass and sank a 21-footer to give us a 60–59 victory.

The other key game was a 55–54 win over University of Utah in Salt Lake City. Utah was ahead 54–51 with less than three minutes to play. Juden Smith forced a turnover and Fred Reynolds scored to make it 54–53, Utah. After the Utes missed a lay-up we went into our four-corner offense. Smith tried a reverse lay-up but missed. However, he was fouled and made both free throws. Utah got two more shots off, but missed.

Talk about coming through in the clutch, these players were experts at it.

Both the New Mexico and the Utah wins are listed by Eddie Mullens in his brochure as two of our all-time most exciting games.

All my players had a good year, but Goodwin was especially outstanding.

We had a freshman on the team who came off the bench and did a good job. He was Hernell Jackson, a six-one guard from Gardena, California. He was nicknamed "Jeep."

We went into the NCAA play-offs having lost only three games all season. We went back up to Salt Lake City for the regional tournament and our first opponent was University of Nevada at Las Vegas.

I really felt our team was at its peak. We were happy, for we hadn't expected to have such an outstanding season. When I say we were happy, I include not only my players but our fans and myself.

You can get too happy. We weren't hungry when we went against UNLV and played poorly. We lost 73–60.

I was very disappointed, despite the fact UNLV had as fine talent as any team in the country. But a team should give it its best shot at that time of year and we didn't. I guess down deep I was probably so happy that I didn't prepare our players well enough.

Forty Seven

IN 1984–85, WE WON twenty-two games and lost ten during the regular season and finished in undisputed first place in the WAC with a record of twelve wins and four losses.

Our first opponent in the NCAA regionals in Albuquerque was Tulsa, coached by my former star, Nolan Richardson.

Nolan's little daughter had been very ill and he had been very preoccupied. In fact, it wasn't even known if he would be at the game. He did show up, but just before the game began.

My players broke a couple of first and second round records, one for most free throw attempts (55) and the other for most free throws made (39) in a single game. We won 79–75.

Richardson became head basketball coach at University of Arkansas soon after that, and I couldn't be happier.

We went up against North Carolina State in the next game and got beat 86–73.

Goodwin and Lockhart were seniors that season and won many games for us.

Goodwin was as pure a shooter as you could ask for. He set a school career record in free throw percentage that may stand for a long time. He made 181 of 221 free throw attempts for a percentage of .819. The previous school record was .790 held by Dick Gibbs.

Goodwin also set a school record for most field goals attempted (1,206) and most field goals made (572). That figures out to a .474 percentage which is pretty amazing considering most of his shots were from way outside.

Lockhart was a good, clean-cut, All-American type of kid — an art major. He was an extremely hard-nosed kid. And a good player inside or out. He made many long-range baskets.

He ranks sixth on UTEP's all-time list for most assists in a single season. He had sixty-three during the 1982–83 season.

The graduation of Goodwin and Lockhart, both guards, would leave us hurting for the next season.

But Jeep Jackson would be a junior. He had shown flashes of being an outstanding player and we planned to move him to point guard the next year.

We had an overtime game this season that we'll remember a long time. We went not one, not two, but three overtimes with Brigham Young University. We finally pulled away and won 97–86.

Forty Eight

IT'S IRONIC, but we played our worst games at the beginning of the season and at the end of the season in 1985–86.

In between we won 27 games. We finished with a 27–6

season record and tied for the WAC championship with a mark of 12–4.

We opened the season against University of Washington and took a terrible licking. I'm sure some people wrote us off for the season after that performance.

I knew we weren't ready for that game. You don't lose your two starting guards, especially of the caliber of Goodwin and Lockhart, and expect to start off well. But frankly, I didn't think we'd get beat that bad. We played as poorly as a team can play.

When we got home after that shellacking we had four days of hard practice. I mean *hard*.

I've got to give the players a lot of credit. They got real determined instead of throwing in the towel. And they started improving.

Feitl and Smith were seniors and our leaders. You can't have a good season if your seniors don't play well and show leadership. They did.

Both were a bit inconsistent, however. It would have been easier if both played well at the same time. Many times it seemed that when Smith had a good game, Feitl didn't. When Feitl had a good game, Smith didn't.

But even having just one of them playing well was a big help. Besides, you can't win 27 games with just one or two players, and they had plenty of help. Quintan Gates had a good season. And Mike Richmond, a six-nine center we got from Hobbs Junior College, developed very quickly. In fact, at one point I considered him the most improved player not only on our team and the WAC, but in the entire country. In December, I would put him in to relieve Feitl only when I had to. Within a few weeks, he could have been a starter. He helped us beat University of New Mexico in Albuquerque, scoring over twenty points.

We went into the NCAA tournament at the end of the season and played another bad game. Bradley beat us 83–58.

We were behind by only two points at the half, but we were already whipped. The refs were calling a lot of picky fouls and Feitl and Smith both had three fouls at halftime. In addition, Jackson fouled out with eight minutes left in the game.

A poor start and a poor ending. Still, twenty-seven wins is a pretty good showing. And I was glad when Feitl went in the second round and Smith in the third round in the NBA draft.

It was a good way to mark my twenty-fifth year as coach of the Miners.

Forty Nine

THE 1986–87 SEASON was one of the most enjoyable of my career. But tragedy struck after it was over.

When you're not picked to do well and you do well, it's really satisfying.

We were picked to finish third in the WAC. And after our opening game, which we lost to Oregon State by eleven points, I didn't think we could win ten games during the season. We looked awful.

But we wound up with a 25–7 season record, won the conference championship with a 13–3 mark and earned a berth in the NCAA Tournament. It was the fifth year in a row we had either won or tied for the WAC title.

We won our first game in the NCAA Tournament, beating University of Arizona on its home court, and then lost by two points to a fine Iowa team.

I got a lot of praise for our success, but the man who should really get the credit is Tim Floyd. He recruited the players on the team before accepting the head coaching job at University of Idaho.

I think the effects of coaching are greatly exaggerated. Coaches get too much praise and too much criticism. Take a major league manager. If his key player hits .350 and the team wins the pennant, the manager is regarded as a genius. But if that player hits .250 and the team loses, then he's seen as a poor manager.

It's the same in basketball. In college, plugging the holes left by graduating seniors is the important thing. We lost Feitl and Smith from the season before but Floyd saw to it that those holes were plugged and I was fortunate that the players he got to plug those holes had a good year.

The main reason we got off to a slow start is that we had a lot of injuries and illness starting out the season. We had so many problems in that department that sometimes we didn't have enough players to scrimmage up and down the floor.

But this was a gritty bunch. That and a busy schedule early in the season helped us get going.

Mike Richmond started out not playing very well but he really came around. He plugged the hole in the middle left by Feitl.

Quintan Gates all of a sudden matured and became a very good player.

Jeep Jackson was excellent the entire year.

Those three were our seniors.

When Chris Sandle, a six feet six transfer from Arizona State, became eligible it really helped. He plugged the gap left by Juden Smith.

Then there was Chris Blocker, a six feet six junior college transfer. He certainly had his moments, making key shots to help us win some games.

Wayne Campbell got better physically and made a great contribution to the team. He had been hobbled by an injury the season before.

Other players on the team were Tim Hardaway, who improved a lot over his freshman season; Antonio Davis, a six-eight freshman who didn't come around from an injury until late in the season; Terry Stallworth, who helped us a lot at guard; Jerry Jones, a six-six freshman who may turn out to be a good player; and Merl Heimer, a six-six freshman from El Paso's Eastwood High.

We were lucky that we had five games in the space of seven days early in December. That got us into physical condition. Included in those four games were two with New Mexico State, which is always a tough opponent.

We went to Georgetown after the New Mexico State games. It was Sandle's first game and we had a chance to win. But we couldn't hit three pointers at the end and lost by four.

I came to the realization that we might have a good team in our next game. It's always tough to win at Lamar University but we went up there and won by sixteen.

We went into the Sun Bowl Tournament and took the championship. Then we opened WAC play at Hawaii and San Diego State. They weren't among the strongest teams in the conference but they were "must" games. We played well and won both.

We came back to El Paso to play Brigham Young University. Sandle got sick before the game and I feel that cost us a win.

He was able to play ten minutes in our next game against Utah and I'm glad of that because we might not have won that game, either.

We lost at Wyoming. Gates got hurt the night before at Colorado State. Had he been well, we might have won.

The only other conference game we lost was at New Mexico, which is understandable. Everybody has a hard time winning there.

We traveled to Utah and beat both Utah and Brigham Young, which put us in good position to win the title.

A lot of people don't realize how tough it is when everybody's shooting at you. That's why it's difficult to repeat as champion in any sport. So I really have to compliment my players for being able to be "up" for as many games as they were. I don't see how they did it.

Tiny Archibald returned "home" to become my assistant. He had tried to get a coaching job in the NBA but hadn't been able to catch on. We hired him to take Floyd's place.

Norm Ellenberger, former New Mexico coach, became a volunteer assistant coach. He had been unable to get into coaching because of some problems he had at New Mexico. Some people may have thought we'd be criticized for letting him help us but I never heard a bad word about it.

Rus Bradburd was my other paid assistant. He helped Floyd with recruiting and he deserves a lot of credit, too.

I'll always remember this year's team. Because the players were over-achievers with a lot of heart, it'll go down as one of my all-time favorites.

One of the most painful tragedies in all my life occurred after the season. Jeep Jackson collapsed and died during an exhibition game. He and some other ex-Miners were playing against a visiting team of Houston Oilers. He died of a heart attack related to a congenital heart ailment.

One of my fondest memories of Jeep is when we cinched the 1987 Western Athletic Conference championship against Wyoming. Immediately after the final buzzer, instead of celebrating with his teammates, he ran into the stands where his mother and father were sitting and hugged them.

Jeep was a leader and a winner and a friendly spirit who was always smiling.

I took his death very hard. I don't know if I'll ever get over it.

Fifty

I'VE GOT TO SAY SOMETHING about the annual Sun Bowl Basketball Tournament.

There's nobody in the country who runs a tournament better than the people who put on the Sun Bowl. I've been to tournaments all over the country, so I feel I know what I'm talking about.

We've had many, many major colleges come to the tournament and the reason is the Sun Bowl committee. They're the greatest hosts in the world. The meet is always around Christmas time and the members of the Sun Bowl take over the visiting teams and show them a great time. Word has gotten around the country and many teams are eager to come to the tournament.

The Sun Bowl not only treats out of town teams well; they've always treated me and my players with the utmost hospitality. And they've been very generous with gifts and other considerations to all participants.

The tournament, incidentally, began the same year I became coach of the Miners. That was 1961. We won that very first one, beating Baylor 70–46 and University of New Mexico 73–65.

And we've had great success in the tournament ever since. We won it a total of sixteen times in the first twenty-five years it was held.

There was only one time we finished worse than third. We lost both games in 1978 and if you remember, that was the year I had all those freshmen.

Because of all the good teams that participate, it's a tough meet in which to win. In December of 1985 Ohio State failed to win a game, but later won the NIT.

We're lucky the meet is played in our Special Events Center. The home advantage is a big asset in all sports, but it's especially so in basketball.

There's one thing I don't like about tournaments, by the way. It's having a breakfast or a luncheon the day of tournament games. No coach I know likes that. Game day is, or should be, a work day. Teams should have time to do the things they must do to prepare.

Outside of that, tournaments can be a lot of fun. And especially the Sun Bowl.

Fifty One

A COUPLE OF THINGS have happened in basketball the last few years that I don't like.

One is post-season conference play-offs to decide a representative in the NCAA meet. The WAC got into the act a few years ago.

What do you accomplish? What are we playing for during the regular season? Everybody goes into the post-season play-offs after the conference race. The league championship is cheapened. It means little or nothing now.

They can say what they want but it's just for a few bucks. Conference officials say they're trying to get two teams into the NCAA tournament. That's a bunch of malarkey.

That and the three-point goal are the dumbest things basketball has ever done.

The three-point goal is ridiculous. I don't think that's college basketball.

We were already drawing big crowds. What do we need it for? The rule as it was must not have been real bad if we were doing as well as we were.

The WAC had been real smart in avoiding that rule, but now the rule has become nationwide.

The new 45-second clock is another thing I'm not exactly overjoyed about. A team with big players has a tremendous advantage.

I'll give you an example. We were playing University of Arizona some years ago. They had about three big players that were going to go in the NBA's first round. We had a small team.

We went into a spread offense. We weren't out to hold the ball; we were out to get them spread out. We scored and beat 'em. We couldn't have done it with a 45-second clock.

I'll give you another example. Say one team is in a zone defense. The other team goes to a half-court offense. It doesn't mean that the latter team is trying to slow the game down. It means it's just trying to make the other team change defense. That's another thing you can't do with a 45-second clock.

Simply, the clock takes coaching out of the game.

I think the fans in El Paso are more knowledgeable than most in other parts of the country. There are a lot of fans who wouldn't stand for a team going into a half-court like we have done. But El Pasoans understood, and they were behind us.

Fifty Two

I'VE BEEN REGARDED as a defensive coach, and that's right.

My philosophy is that defense wins in any sport. Just look at the year 1986.

The Chicago Bears won the Super Bowl. Why? Defense.

The Kansas City Royals won the World Series. Why? Defense.

The Boston Celtics won the NBA championship. Why? Defense.

I've been asked what I look for in a player so far as defense goes. I answer that defense is a team thing.

We've had some great individual defensive players but what we look for is players who are willing to work hard together. Defense is hard, hard work. Defense is five people learning to play together.

If one man doesn't play well it won't work. If the player

165

guarding the ball isn't working any harder than the other four trying to help him, you can forget it.

It's a philosophy that I learned from Henry Iba. I saw it worked and I came to be a believer in it.

There are many coaches who have learned the same philosophy. That's what makes coaching so tough now. You don't find teams that are poorly coached anymore. There are too many clinics, too many seminars, too many smart people in the ranks.

These new young coaches are something. They all have three-piece suits, they're ambitious and they're willing to work hard.

I never used to think I'd use a zone defense. I played man to man with no switching under Mr. Iba and I loved it.

I never even used to work on it in practice.

But I've had to adjust, and I think we play it pretty well.

I started putting in the zone in practices some years ago and found it worked, especially against good perimeter players. There are a lot of those around now and they force you to play a zone.

Speaking of players, there are so many good ones now that it's unbelievable. There are players in high school now who can't get on a college team who would have been starters ten years ago.

And I guess there'll be more of them, and even better ones, ten years from now.

Another of my coaching philosophies has to do with high schools. We look for players who come from winning high school teams. There are exceptions, but we've found that players develop habits early, and winning can be one of them. Most of our successful teams have been made up of players who were winners in high school.

166

Fifty Three

NO ONE CAN MAKE IT in the coaching business without the support of his family, and I've been lucky in that respect.

My wife, Mary, encouraged me to get into coaching while I was still playing. And ever since I got into it, my entire family has been super supportive.

I'm so aware of this need that when I hire an assistant coach I'm just as anxious to talk to the wife as I am to the coach. A coach's wife who wants her man home by five o'clock every day will be in trouble.

I've been very lucky, because the wives of my assistant coaches have been understanding. Beverly Floyd, Tim's wife, was a good example. Tim would be gone for twenty days at a time recruiting and there was never any crying or bellyaching. And that's why he's got such a good chance to do well. He's got the backing.

I know a lot of men who are no longer coaching because they didn't get that type of support.

I've been lucky with my four sons. A couple of them were pretty good golfers. Steve seemed to have a bright future in the game but he hurt his back when he was eighteen years old. He was attending New Mexico State and got injured piddling around with wrestling. But he's playing again and doing well.

167

I don't want to say too much about my sons because I know they wouldn't like it. But just let me say that my four sons turned out to be good people.

My younger brother Jerry (he and I were the only children in our family) was not only a great athlete but a genius.

He was recruited by just about every football college in the country. He wound up at University of Oklahoma.

He pitched nine no-hitters in American Legion baseball and high school, too.

He was starting fullback at Oklahoma as a freshman but ended up going into the Marines the next year. He didn't like school.

He was always building something. And he could do anything with cars. If anything happens to my car, I'm lost. Not him. He could take one apart and put it back together even when he was in high school.

When I was in college and he was a junior in high school, he made a submachine gun from scratch. He got different parts, put them together, welded them and it worked.

Later, he invented a short bolt rifle that became very popular. He didn't make much out of it. He sold the patent for about $30,000.

He invented so many other things that he has only two less inventions than Browning, the world renowned rifle company. His guns have been featured in *Gun Digest*.

During the past five years, he invented a sniper rifle that the Armed Forces bought.

He's living now in Rogers, Arkansas. I don't know what he's up to now. He's a genius, like I said, and has so many things going I can't keep up with him.

Fifty Four

ONE OF MY BIGGEST REGRETS ever is that I stopped a lawsuit against James Michener, the author who wrote *Sports in America*.

He repeated the mistakes about our 1966 team that *Sports Illustrated* had printed.

Michener's book is now being looked upon as an "authoritative" record on the history of sports in the United States and I'm afraid some people might believe the errors about us.

Michener may be regarded by some as the world's greatest researcher. But I don't think he is. I don't think he did much researching about our 1966 team. He apparently just accepted what was printed in *Sports Illustrated*.

He may be a good writer, but what he repeated about us is a bunch of baloney.

He even repeated that none of our black players' wives could get a job in El Paso. Like I pointed out before, none of our players was married.

I'll tell you what a fine group of young men our 1966 players were. Pat Riley, the coach of the Los Angeles Lakers who I mentioned in the first chapter, played for University of Kentucky against us in the finals of the NCAA tournament in 1966. In an interview on him and other players on that Kentucky team it came out that the graduation rate among the Kentucky players of the season was about the same as the graduation rate on our team of that season.

I've always been proud of the graduation rate of my players. I've never failed to preach to them the importance of attending classes. If they don't go to class, they don't practice. And if they don't practice, they don't get to play much. Consequently, we have been ranked among the top schools in the country when it comes to graduating basketball players. Our 1966 team lived up to that tradition.

Most of the 1966 Kentucky players went on to become fine, successful people. And so did our players.

Our 1966 team had a twenty-year reunion in 1986. An El Paso business man, Joe Gomez, brought all the players to El Paso. Another El Pasoan, John Silverman, presented them rings, something they never got when they won the national title.

Just for the record, I am going to list how the twelve players on our 1966 team who were maligned as "outlaws" and were pictured as being "exploited" turned out:

DAVID LATTIN — Public relations, Houston, Texas.

ORSTEN ARTIS — Detective, Gary, Indiana.

HARRY FLOURNOY — Manager, Continental Bakery, Los Angeles, California.

NEVIL SHED — Assistant coach, University of Texas at San Antonio, San Antonio, Texas.

BOBBY JOE HILL — Expediter in Purchasing Department, El Paso Natural Gas Co., El Paso, Texas.

WILLIE WORSLEY — Resident director, Lakeside High School, Spring Valley, New York.

WILLIE CAGER — Head basketball coach, Tornillo High School, Tornillo, Texas.

DICK MYERS — Vice President of operations, Farah Manufacturing Co., El Paso, Texas.

JERRY ARMSTRONG — Basketball coach, King City, Missouri.

DAVID PALACIO — Vice President, Capitol Records, Los Angeles, California.

TOGO RAILEY — Basketball coach, Port Neches-Grove (Texas) High School.

LOUIS BAUDOIN — Art teacher, Albuquerque Academy, Albuquerque, New Mexico.

One of the reasons I'm glad I'm doing this book is so people will have in print the truth about these fine men.

Maybe I should have waited until I retire, but I don't plan to do that any time soon. In fact, I've enjoyed coaching so much, and the people of El Paso have been so good to me, that I hope I'm still coaching the Miners twenty-six years from now.

THE DON HASKINS 26-YEAR FILE

*The only coach to win five Western Athletic Conference championships in a row.

*Guided his team to the 1970 WAC championship the first year the Miners were eligible after joining the conference.

*Won the 1966 NCAA national basketball championship.

*Has had twelve teams at UTEP win at least twenty games.

*Has carried the Miners to ten NCAA tournaments and six at the NIT.

*Long ago became the winningest coach in UTEP history.

*The only coach ever to bring an NCAA basketball championship to the State of Texas.

*Named District XIII Kodak Coach of the Year several times.

*His first twenty-six UTEP teams won 493 games and lost 215.

*Inducted into the Texas Sports Hall of Fame in 1987.

*YEAR BY YEAR RECORDS

Year	School	Won	Lost
1955–56	Benjamin High School	29	10
1956–57	Hedley High School	28	5
1957–58	Hedley High School	31	6
1958–59	Hedley High School	30	7
1959–60	Hedley High School	26	6
1960–61	Dumas High School	25	7
1961–62	Texas Western College	18	6

1962–63	Texas Western College	19	7
1963–64	Texas Western College	25	3
1964–65	Texas Western College	18	9
1965–66	Texas Western College	28	1
1966–67	Texas Western College	22	6
1967–68	Univ. of Texas at El Paso	14	9
1968–69	Univ. of Texas at El Paso	16	9
1970–71	Univ. of Texas at El Paso	17	8
1970–71	Univ. of Texas at El Paso	15	10
1971–72	Univ. of Texas at El Paso	21	7
1972–73	Univ. of Texas at El Paso	16	10
1973–74	Univ. of Texas at El Paso	18	7
1974–75	Univ. of Texas at El Paso	20	6
1975–76	Univ. of Texas at El Paso	20	7
1976–77	Univ. of Texas at El Paso	11	15
1977–78	Univ. of Texas at El Paso	10	16
1978–79	Univ. of Texas at El Paso	11	15
1979–80	Univ. of Texas at El Paso	20	8
1980–81	Univ. of Texas at El Paso	18	12
1981–82	Univ. of Texas at El Paso	20	8
1982–83	Univ. of Texas at El Paso	19	10
1983–84	Univ. of Texas at El Paso	27	4
1984–85	Univ. of Texas at El Paso	22	10
1985–86	Univ. of Texas at El Paso	27	6
1986–87	Univ. of Texas at El Paso	25	7

*Records kept and compiled by UTEP Sports Information Office.

PUBLISHER'S ACKNOWLEDGMENT: To our good friend Joe Gomez, the ultimate basketball enthusiast, whose dynamic energy was instrumental in bringing together the 1966 Texas Western College NCAA Champions for their twenty-year reunion in El Paso. He also gave many hours of his time and talents in proofreading the galleys of this book as well as contacting the 1966 champions to get their autographs for the limited collectors edition of Haskins: The Bear Facts.